W9-BBD-457

LORDS OF SPEECH

Portraits of Fifteen American Orators

LORDS OF SPEECH

Portraits of Fifteen American Orators

by

EDGAR DEWITT JONES

Essay Index Reprint Series

BOOKS FOR LIBRARIES PRESS
FREEPORT, NEW YORK

STANDARD BOOK NUMBER:

8369-1040-0

LIBRARY OF CONGRESS CATALOG CARD NUMBER:

68-58799

PRINTED IN THE UNITED STATES OF AMERICA

To
My Brother
William Westbrook Jones
who loves the music of speech
and delights in the witchery of words

FOREWORD

THIS BOOK does not pretend to be a history of American oratory. It is a series of studies of fifteen "bright particular stars" which bespangle the oratorical skies of one hundred and fifty years of a nation's history. The volume begins with Patrick Henry and ends with Woodrow Wilson, and between these two masters of language are thirteen other men who were mighty in speech. They are taken from the hustings, the bar, the pulpit, and the lecture platform, and presented in brief biographical settings. But their speech is the thing.

Geographically, the south has been most fertile in eloquent sons; particularly was this true before and during the Civil War and for a short period thereafter. It is a popular theory that southern climate, soft languorous winds and genial weather inspire silvery eloquence. Yet, the splendidly rhetorical Robert G. Ingersoll was not a southerner, but a middle westerner born in the east; and Seargent S. Prentiss, called " the most eloquent of all southerners," was a New Englander by birth, and a Mississippian only by residence. If there is anything in the theory that a salubrious climate, luxuriant foliage and profusion of flowers produce eloquence, California and Florida should be prolific in the production of orators; but these states are not exceptional in this respect.

From bleak New England came James Otis, Daniel

Webster, the Adamses, Wendell Phillips, Phillips Brooks and Rufus Choate; from the middle west came Ingersoll, Owen Lovejoy, Stephen A. Douglas, Thomas Corwin, Lincoln, Daniel W. Voorhees, Benjamin Harrison, A. J. Beveridge, the elder LaFollette and Frances E. Willard; from Virginia, Kentucky, Tennessee, the Carolinas and other southern states came William L. Yancey, John C. Calhoun, John C. Breckinridge, Robert Y. Haynes, John J. Crittenden and Booker T. Washington.

Perhaps the time is fully come to recall to a generation which professes not to be greatly interested in oratory the place and power of eloquence in the American scene. There were oratorical giants in the golden age of oratory; there are many able speakers in our own times, and the age of powerful public speaking has not passed.

Carelessness on the part of those who speak in public — shoddy sentences, commonplace phrasings, inaccurate use of words — sins against good taste, and is an affront to the auditors. The mastery of an excellent style of private or public speech is achieved only by tireless study, much writing, the hardest kind of toil. Some years ago the writer served for two weeks as a juror in the Recorder's Court of his city. The speeches of the lawyers provided profitable study. For the most part they were dull, uninteresting, badly arranged, and the language was evidently extempore. Occasionally a lawyer would appear whose speech was markedly different — concise, logical, carefully prepared. Invariably when this occurred the courtroom came to life; the judge, who had been covertly reading a newspaper, raised his eyes from the sheet; the jury awakened as men out of sleep.

And what should be said of ministers of religion, men privileged to speak upon the most important themes of life, who come into the pulpit with poorly prepared sermons, platitudinous statements, sentences that no one could possibly parse? One thing that differentiates poor from good preaching is the bare mechanics of it — the choice of language, the use of illustrations, the preparation and the vocabulary. Good diction may not be the most important thing in preaching but certainly it is not the least important.

The golden age of the orator is gone, but the era of good public speaking is here to stay. The style and manner of oratory changes, yet true eloquence persists. There will always be a place for the public speaker who has something to say and says it effectively. The radio has put a premium on careful preparation, clear enunciation, brevity and good diction, and it has been proved that the invisible speaker can convey his personality over the air. Yet at its best the radio speech can never quite equal the power of the spoken word when it is mediated through the physical presence of a powerful orator.

It has been claimed by a competent critic that " a great oration is the very flower of literature," and there is much in the annals of eloquence to sustain this claim. An excursion into the story of American oratory is a venture into a rhetorical Elysium where men speak with the tongues of angels.

E. DeW. J.

DETROIT, MICHIGAN

CONTENTS

PATRICK HENRY

The Tongue of the Revolution

I

PATRICK HENRY

THE FAME of no other great orator rests upon literary evidence so slight as that which witnesses to "the tongue of the Revolution," Patrick Henry. He left no manuscripts or published volumes of the speeches which stirred Virginia and her sister colonies like the strident notes of a bugle. Or if he did leave manuscripts they were lost or destroyed. For the one speech that has come down in fullest form, the "Give me liberty or give me death" oration, some contemporaries contend the text is incomplete and that as originally delivered it was still more eloquent and powerful. The argument presents fruit for interesting speculation, since that speech, as we have it, seems complete and packed with rhetorical dynamite. Contemporaries declare that no pen could follow Henry when he was in full swing, that the reporters lost themselves in the torrent of his eloquence.

Henry's fame rests largely upon hearsay, and of such evidence Virginia was filled to overflowing for a generation after the orator's death. Contemporary letters, diaries, newspapers and memoirs teem with accounts, anecdotes and tributes attesting to the spell the mighty Patrick cast over his auditors. But what would we not give for, say, a half dozen manuscripts of his best known speeches? It is odd that he did not leave such a legacy. He came of a literary line, read prodigiously, spent much time in his library preparing legal arguments and forensic addresses. The disappearance of his manuscripts is a mystery that has not been cleared up. And this very fact helps to account for Henry's unique place in the hall of fame.

William Wirt, Henry's first biographer, and for years the only one, was himself an orator. His invaluable Life of Henry is an oratorical biography if there ever was one; its hero is never out of platform character. It is Wirt to whom we are indebted for excerpts from Henry's best known oratorical triumphs, particularly his arguments in the British Debts case, apparently taken from stenographic notes by court reporters. Wirt relates that in the course of Henry's second argument in the British Debts case Judge Iredell, one of the sitting jurists, exclaimed: " Gracious God! He is an orator indeed." This outburst is strong enough, it would appear, but Wirt hastens to state that the argument which elicited it was inferior to that of the first speech.

Patrick Henry was born not far from Richmond in Hanover County, Virginia, on May 29, 1736. His boyhood was perfectly normal, that of a healthy young pagan loving the out-of-doors. He went barefoot in summer time, fished, swam, did chores, roamed the forest in the fall and winter with his flintlock. He clerked in a country store; read more widely than most boys of the neighborhood; married Sarah Shelton; tried farming with indifferent success; studied law in a desultory fashion, and by the skin of his teeth was admitted to the bar. From comparative obscurity he emerged a celebrity. Six terms he served as governor of Virginia. He was twice married, his second wife being Dorothea Dandridge, and he was the father of seventeen children in all. His first great speech was made in 1763, when he appeared in the famous Parsons' case and fulminated against the established clergy and the perquisites which they claimed were theirs under the crown. The rumble of revolution was in that speech. It smacked of treason and put the name of Patrick Henry on the tongues of a multitude.

Henry's second notable speech was inspired by the obnoxious Stamp Act. The old capitol at Williamsburg (long since demolished), where the young orator thrilled his hearers, has been reconstructed, along with a dozen other historic buildings. The session destined to be immortalized by Henry was tumultuous. The air was electric, charged with revolt. Only a fragment of the orator's speech has come down to us — the dramatic conclusion. Those who heard it never forgot the flaming climax. In a voice and with a manner that startled even those who knew of his masterful tongue, Henry thundered: " Tarquin and Caesar had each his Brutus, Charles I his Cromwell, and George III — " He paused. " Treason! " came a shout from the speaker high on his dais. " Treason! " " Treason! " cried many Burgesses. Henry stood statuesque in an eloquent pause. His whole being seemed to expand. There was a lofty light in his eyes. With a calmness

that was ominous, he spoke his final words: " — and
George III may profit by their example! If *this* be
treason make the most of it! "

Patrick Henry was a natural orator, not a trained
rhetorician. He possessed the fire and fury without
the finesse and the artistry of the elocutionist. He is
described as a little under six feet in height, slender,
and of disposition mild until aroused. Then his stoop-
ing shoulders straightened, his deep blue eyes became
black and blazing. Of his voice someone has said: " He
could make love in a corner, or call a hound a mile
away." He invariably wore a wig in public and, while
ordinarily careless in dress, was accustomed to appear
in court or on occasions of moment wearing a scarlet
coat flung over black velvet smallclothes. He usually
began his speeches in a low tone, often appearing to
be indisposed or ailing, or giving the impression that
he was not prepared; and then suddenly he would fling
forth a torrent of strong, ringing sentences and pictorial paragraphs, words tumbling over words like a
cataract, pausing only when the pause would be effective. Thus he would storm and persuade, berate
and beg, threaten and cajole, argue and amuse, convince and convulse — a magnetic master of popular
assemblies.

There was the celebrated and ludicrous case of John
Hook, a Tory storekeeper of New London. When the
American soldiers were suffering for food during the
Cornwallis invasion, the commissary of the Continental
Army seized two of Hook's steers. After peace had
been restored, Hook brought action of trespass against

the commissary. Henry appeared for the defendant and made a laughingstock out of poor Hook, carrying the jury and his hearers with his unbridled imagination. In a series of swift strokes he pictured the distresses of the American army, exposed, almost naked, to the rigor of a winter sky, and marking with the blood of their unshod feet the frozen ground over which they marched. " Where was the man," he cried, " who had an American heart in his bosom, who would not have thrown open his fields, his barns, his cellars, the doors of his house, the portals of his breast, to receive with open arms the meanest soldier in that little band of famished patriots? Where is the man? There he stands! " he exclaimed, pointing out the embarrassed plaintiff, and while the eyes of the people were fastened upon Hook, Henry dilated on the joys of the people when victory came to the American arms. Then he shouted: " But hark! What notes of discord are these which disturb the general joy and silence the affirmations of victory? They are the notes of John Hook hoarsely bawling through the American camp: ' Beef! Beef! Beef! ' "

But the jury found for the plaintiff and assessed the defendant one penny damages.

St. John's Church still stands on Richmond Hill, and is but little changed since that momentous day in March, 1775. Richmond was a small city then, of four thousand population, and that church was the only available meeting place for the provincial convention that was to bring the state of Virginia to war with Great Britain. It was crowded to the limit on that day of days and eager-eyed patriots stood outside looking in through the open windows and doors, for the weather was warm and pleasant. In the pulpit of St. John's sat Peyton Randolph, president of the convention. The delegates faced him, looking east. Henry, then in his thirty-ninth year, sat in the third pew on the north side. Two opposing parties were meeting in this convention; one was made up of those who favored postponement of drastic action, and the other of those who believed the time had come to resort to arms. In all, one hundred and twenty-two men who were to mold history sat in that convention — the radical leaders of the colonies.

President Randolph called on the Reverend Miles Selden, who offered prayer. The minutes of the previous meeting were read and approved. Mr. Edmund Pendleton of Caroline County presented a resolution thanking the assembly of the Island of Jamaica " for the exceeding generous and affectionate part they have so nobly taken in the unhappy contest between Great Britain and her colonies." Mr. Robert Carter Nicholas seconded the resolution, which was adopted.

Patrick Henry of Hanover then offered two resolutions: " Resolved that a well regulated militia is the natural strength and only security of a free government. . . . That this colony be immediately put into a state of defense. . . ." Richard Henry Lee seconded the resolutions, saying, " I think they are timely and highly important." Benjamin Harrison from Charles County voiced opposition, calling the resolutions " rash and inexpedient." Thomas Jefferson spoke in favor:

" I regard these acts of Parliament — attempting to tax our people and shutting up the port of Boston — as the acts of a foreign power which should, by all means in our power, be resisted." Mr. Pendleton spoke again in opposition: " I hope this convention will proceed slowly before rushing the country into war." Mr. Nicholas agreed with Mr. Pendleton: " I consider the resolution of the gentleman from Hanover as hasty, rash, and unreasonable." Mr. Thomas Nelson from York County, a merchant, supported the resolution. George Washington of Fairfax also supported Henry. " I am a soldier," he said, " and believe in being prepared. I will raise one thousand men, subsist them at my own expense, and march myself at their head to the relief of Boston." Patrick Henry of Hanover addressed the chair and was recognized. The great moment had come:

No man thinks more highly than I do of the patriotism as well as the abilities of the very honorable gentlemen who have just addressed the house. But different men often see the same subject in different lights; and, therefore, I hope it will not be thought disrespectful to these gentlemen, if, entertaining as I do opinions of a character opposite to theirs, I should speak forth my sentiments freely and without reserve. This is no time for ceremony. The question before the house is one of awful moment to this country. For my own part, I consider it as nothing less than a question of freedom or slavery; and in proportion to the magnitude of the subject ought to be the freedom of the debate. It is only in this way that we can hope to arrive at truth and fulfill the great responsibility which we owe to God and our country. Should I keep back my opinions at such a time, through fear of giving offense, I should consider myself as guilty of treason toward my country, and of an act of disloyalty toward the majesty of heaven, which I revere above all earthly kings.

Mr. President: It is natural for man to indulge in the illusions of hope. We are apt to shut our eyes against a painful truth — and listen to the song of that siren till she transforms us into beasts. Is this the part of wise men engaged in a great and arduous struggle for liberty? Are we disposed to be of the number of those who, having eyes, see not, and having ears, hear not, the things which so nearly concern their temporal salvation? For my part, whatever anguish of spirit it might cost, I am willing to know the whole truth; to know the worst and to provide for it. . . .

Observe the serenity of these opening paragraphs, how winsome, persuasive and reasonable they are. Contrast the leisurely movement and calm spirit with the passion, vehemence and fire of the closing paragraphs. The orator has been speaking but a few minutes. He has passed from the winsome note of the introduction through a series of bristling interrogations as to the wisdom of further delay, and on to a terrific indictment of Great Britain and her attitude of oppression. Fully aroused, master of himself and of his audience, he roared like a lion:

We must fight. I repeat it, sir, we *must* fight. An appeal to arms and to the God of hosts is all that is left us. . . . They tell us, sir, that we are weak — unable to cope with so formidable an adversary. But when shall we be stronger? Will it be the next week, or the next year? Will it be when we are totally disarmed, and when a British guard shall be stationed in every house? Shall we gather strength by irresolution and inaction? Shall we acquire the means of effectual resistance by lying supinely on our backs, and hugging the delusive phantom of hope, until our enemies shall have bound us hand and foot?

Sir, we are not weak, if we make a proper use of those means which the God of nature hath placed in our power. Three millions of people, armed in the holy cause of liberty, and in such a country as that which we possess, are invincible to any force which our enemy can send against us. Besides, sir, we shall not fight our battles alone. There is a just God who presides over the destinies of nations, and who will raise up friends to fight our battles for us. The battle, sir, is not to the strong alone; it is to the vigilant, the active, the brave. Besides, sir, we have no election. If we were base enough to desire it, it is now too late to retire from the contest. There is no retreat but in submission and slavery. Our chains are forged. Their clanking may be heard on the plains of Boston. The war is inevitable. And let it come! I repeat it, sir: let it come!

It is in vain, sir, to extenuate the matter. Gentlemen may cry peace, peace — but there is no peace. The war is actually begun! The next gale that sweeps from the north will bring to our ears the clash of resounding arms! Our brethren are already in the field! Why stand we idle here? What is it that gentlemen wish? What would they have? Is life so dear, or peace so sweet, as to be purchased at the price of chains and slavery? Forbid it, Almighty God! I know not what course others may take, but as for me, give me liberty or give me death!

A Baptist clergyman who was present has left his impressions of the orator on this historic occasion: " Henry arose with an unearthly fire burning in his eye. He commenced somewhat calmly — but smothered excitement began to play more and more upon his features, and thrill in the tones of his voice. The tendons of his neck stood out white and rigid like whipcords. His voice rose louder and louder, until the walls of the building and all within them seemed to shake and rock in its tremendous vibrations. Finally his pale face and glaring eyes became terrible to look upon. Men leaned forward in their seats with their heads strained forward, their faces pale, and their eyes glaring like the speaker's. His last exclamation — ' Give me liberty, or give me death! ' — was like the shout of a leader who turns back the rout of battle. When he sat down I felt sick with excitement. Every eye yet gazed entranced on Henry. It seemed as if a word from him would have led to any wild explosion of violence. Men looked beside themselves.''

John Roane, another spectator, has left a vivid account of this philippic: '' He stood like a Roman senator defying Caesar, while the unconquerable spirit of Cato of Utica flashed from every feature, and he closed the grand appeal with the solemn words, ' or give me death! ' which sounded with the awful cadence of a hero's dirge . . . and he suited the action to the word by a blow upon the left breast with the right hand, which seemed to drive the dagger to the patriot's heart.''

Oratorically there is but one opinion on this speech; but as to another aspect the following comment by Christopher Hollis in *The American Heresy* makes interesting reading:

'' Such language is intolerable. War is so great an evil that when it and peace are in the balance no man has the right to use rhetoric, whose sole purpose is to rob its hearers of reason. Even at this distance of time an honorable reader must feel ashamed when he comes across this speech, yet because of it, Virginia by a vote of sixty-five to sixty and the advice of Jefferson and Washington, committed herself to preparations for war. The die was cast. In the next month war broke out in Massachusetts; at Lexington the first blood was shed."

Mr. Hollis is an Englishman!

The twenty-fifth of November, 1791, saw the capital of Virginia astir with excitement. Patrick Henry was to appear in Federal Circuit Court in the suit of William Jones, a British subject, against Dr. Thomas Walker, an American citizen, in what is known as the British Debts case. Dr. Thomas was being sued for non-payment of a bond which bore a date previous to the revolutionary war. It was a test case, and attracted international attention. The legal issue involved was itself an interesting one, and the suit important because of the precedent it would establish. By the treaty of 1783, America agreed that the British debts should be recoverable here. Under the Constitution that treaty became the supreme law of the land. But on October 20, 1777, Virginia acting as a sovereign state had directed that money due British subjects be paid into her treasury. On May 3, 1779, the legislature passed an act of forfeiture, vesting all British property in the commonwealth. These laws had been made prior to the making of either the treaty or the Constitution.

However, it was the appearance of Patrick Henry for the defendant that set Richmond agog and filled her streets and taverns with excited citizens. By courtesy of the court the usual regulations were set aside. Visitors filled vacant seats on the benches and occupied every inch of available space. Scores stood about the walls; others failing to gain admission were permitted to stand in the corridors, while outside the capitol a disappointed multitude lingered for a glimpse of Patrick Henry and whiled away the hours with tales of his oratorical prowess and the probable outcome of the case.

Within, the confusion of getting settled gradually subsided. The courtroom became quiet. The moment was tense. All eyes were on Patrick Henry, who slowly rose to his feet. In his fifty-seventh year, he looked older. He actually seemed feeble. He stooped a little, yet he made an impressive figure. For this occasion he was dressed in a suit of dignified black cloth with conspicuous velvet trimming. Over his dark smallclothes was flung a scarlet cloak. His brown wig was powdered and tied with a broad black satin ribbon. He wore spectacles, which he fingered as he began to speak. His voice at first was scarcely audible beyond the first half dozen rows of seats, but soon it filled the room melodiously. At first he appeared ill at ease, and gave the impression of timidity, as though this was not an old but a novel experience on which he was about to venture.

A long pause . . . Patrick Henry was speaking: *

" I stand here, may it please your honors, to support, according to my power, that side of the question which respects the American debtor."

Another pause.

* The excerpts that follow are from William Wirt's *Sketches of the Life and Character of Patrick Henry* (ninth edition).

I beg leave to beseech the patience of this honorable court; because the subject is very great and important, and because I have not only the greatness of the subject to consider, but those numerous observations which have come from the opposing counsel to answer. Thus, therefore, the matter proper for my discussion is unavoidably accumulated. Sir, there is a circumstance in this case that is more to be deplored than that which I have just mentioned, and that is this: those animosities which the injustice of the British nation hath produced, and which I had well hoped would never again be the subject of discussion, are necessarily brought forth.

The orator's flow of language was better now, smoother, faster. A vibrancy crept into his voice. He straightened his shoulders, lifted his chin, gestured with more grace and ease. His magic tones filled the room:

The conduct of that nation, which bore so hard upon us in the late contest, becomes once more the subject of investigation. I know, sir, how well it becomes a liberal man and a Christian to forget and to forgive. As individuals professing a holy religion, it is our bounden duty to forgive injuries done us as individuals. But when to the character of Christian you add the character of patriot, you are in a different situation. Our mild and holy system of religion inculcates an admirable maxim of forbearance. If your enemy smite one cheek, turn the other to him. But you must stop there. You cannot apply this to your country. As members of a social community, this maxim does not apply to you. When you consider injuries done to your country, your political duty tells you of vengeance. Forgive as a private man, but never forgive public injuries. Observations of this nature are exceedingly unpleasant, but it is my duty to use them. . . .

America was a sovereign nation when her sons stepped forth to resist the unjust hand of oppression, and declared themselves independent. The consent of Great Britain was not necessary (as the gentlemen on the other side urge) to create us a nation.

Yes, sir, we were a nation, long before the monarch of that little island in the Atlantic ocean gave his puny assent to it. [These words he accompanied by a most significant gesture — rising on tiptoe, pointing as to a vast distance, and half closing his eyes, as if endeavoring with extreme difficulty to draw a sight on some object almost too small for vision, and blowing out the words " puny assent " with lips curled with unutterable contempt.]

Can any gentleman show me any instance where the life or property of a gentleman or plebeian in England is forfeited, and yet his debts spared? The state can claim debts due to one guilty of high treason. Are they not subject to confiscation? I concur in that sound principle, that good faith is essential to the happiness of mankind; that its want stops all human intercourse and renders us miserable. This principle is permanent and universal. Look to what point of the compass you will, you will find it pervading all nations. Who does not set down its sacred influence as the only thing that comforts human life? *Does the plaintiff claim through good faith?* How does *he* derive his claim? *Through* perfidy: through a *polluted channel.* Everything of that kind would have come better from our side of the question than from theirs. . . .

Sir, it was not done in a corner. It was understood by our enemies. They had a right to retaliate on any species of our property they could find. The right of retaliation or just retortion, for equivalent damage on any part of an enemy's property, is permitted to every nation. What right has the British nation (for if the nation have not the right, none of its people have) to demand a breach of faith in the American government to its citizens? I have already mentioned the engagement of the government with its citizens respecting the paper money — *If you take it, it shall be money.* Shall it be judged now not to be money? Shall this compact be broken for the sake of the British nation? No, sir, the language of national law is otherwise.*

* The writer personally examined in Richmond, Virginia (August, 1934), the brief prepared by Patrick Henry in this celebrated British Debts case. The document is yellow with age and apparently had not been

It was over. Patrick Henry sank into a chair, a spare, crumpled figure, all the fire gone out of him, a spent eagle in scarlet and black. The session was ended. Amid a muffled babble of voices the people poured out of the capitol into the great square. There they mingled with those who were unable to get into the courtroom, and repeated the story of what had happened inside. And practically everyone tarried until Patrick Henry himself, looking small and unutterably weary, appeared. They greeted him with rousing cheers.

Henry's last speech was made early in the spring preceding his death, which occurred June 6, 1799. He spoke in the open at Charlotte on county court day, the first Monday in March. He was introduced by James Adams in this quaint fashion: " Oyez! Oyez! Colonel Henry will address the people from this stand, for the last time, and at the risk of his life." Infirm and deathly white, the old orator looked scarcely able to raise his voice. He began in a low, weak tone, not audible more than a few feet away. But shortly a transformation took place, affecting his whole being as he warmed to his theme. He stood erect, his eyes flashed fire, and the grand voice rang out clear and melodious. He pleaded for unity and tolerance in the distracted electorate. As he concluded, he clasped his hands and swayed from side to side, his audience unconsciously swaying with him. " Let us," he cried, " trust God and our better judgment to set us right hereafter. United we stand: divided we fall. Let us

disturbed since it was filed in the archives of the clerk of the U. S. District Court one hundred and forty-five years ago.

not split into factions which must destroy this union upon which our existence depends. Let us preserve our strength for the French, the English, the Germans, or whoever else shall dare to invade our territory, and not exhaust it in civil commotions and intensive wars."

Friends took Patrick Henry in their arms, and bore him to a room, and tenderly laid him down, for he was badly spent. Then it was that Dr. Rice, a bystander, remarked, " The sun has set in all its glory! "

And so it had.

HENRY CLAY

America's Greatest Natural Orator

HENRY CLAY

IN THE YEAR 1777 Baptist parsonages in Virginia, or for that matter anywhere else, were not manses but plain shelters for big families and bigger problems. This particular parsonage was already populated by four husky youngsters when, on the twelfth of April, another boy was born. The father, who died after two more brothers had been added to the family, was an ardent admirer of Patrick Henry, and the fifth boy's name was probably decided upon before he arrived. His mother had the good sense, and the good luck, to make an admirable second marriage, notwithstanding she had given hostages to fortune seven times over. And the tow-headed Henry, wide-eyed and wider-mouthed, was given a lift fameward by his stepfather, Captain Henry Watkins, who secured for him a clerkship in the office of the Court of High Chancery in Richmond. There he came under the influence of the famous George Wythe, who tutored John Marshall and Thomas Jefferson in law, and who took a great fancy to this young Virginian with the shock of blond hair and the expansive mouth.

Clay went to Kentucky in 1797, and was successful from the first as lawyer and in politics. He went up like a rocket — and stayed up. He was elected to the United States Senate in 1806, before he was thirty years of age. He served six terms in the House of Representatives, and as many terms as speaker. He was elected to five full terms in the United States Senate, was a peace commissioner to Ghent in 1814, and secretary of state in John Quincy Adams' cabinet.

Clay was tall, slender and lean of flank. His grayish blue eyes " seemed to take all hues of that color, from the light and sparkling, to the deep sea blue; now shining as ' the glittering eye ' of the Ancient Mariner, now intense and ' darkly deeply beautiful blue.' " His head was large, over seven inches in diameter (he wore a seven and five-eighths hat) , his complexion ruddy and healthy, his nose large and blunt and his mouth prodigious. And such a voice! But let a contemporary describe it: " No orator's voice superior to his in quality, in compass and management has, we venture to say, been raised upon this continent. It touched every note in the whole gamut of human susceptibilities; it was sweet and soft, as a mother's to her babe. It could be made to float into the chambers of the air, as gently as descending snowflakes on the sea; and again it shook the Senate, strong, brain-shaking, filling the air with its absolute thunder."

As an orator Henry Clay ranks with the greatest of eloquent Americans. If he lacked the grandeur of Webster, he possessed more charm. His power over an audience was extraordinary. In the midst of a speech his whole being became transfigured, his face suffused with a light that seemed unearthly, and there streamed from him invisible currents of magnetism. Tall and willowy, he had a habit of moving about, stepping from side to side during the delivery of a speech, and every little movement had a meaning of its own. While speaking he would sometimes pause and take a pinch of snuff with such grace that it seemed to add to the effectiveness of his delivery. In my college days in Transylvania, Lexington, I met and talked with an old lady who as a little girl had listened to Henry Clay. " He looked and spoke like a god," she said. " He took my hand, held it, and talked to me." " Spoke like a god " — one can believe it. Of our generation William Jennings Bryan alone approached this silver-tongued statesman in popular appeal.

Someone remarked that Clay's mouth looked like the stone mouth of the great Sphinx. An amusing legend has grown up about it. It was said that in the great old days, when men crowded around him to press his hand and women besought him for a patriarchal kiss, his capacity for gratifying the latter demand was un- limited, for the ample dimensions of his mouth enabled him to rest one side of it while the other side was in ac- tive duty. If the women had voted in Clay's time not even General Jackson could have defeated him.

As a specimen of Clay's eloquence, the closing para- graph from his speech in the United States Senate, February 6 and 7, 1850, in behalf of a compromise meas- ure that would avoid dissolution of the union, makes impressive reading. Clay is appalled by thoughts of disunion:

Can you, Mr. President, lightly contemplate the consequences? Can you yield yourself to a torrent of passion, amid dangers which I have depicted in colors far short of what would be the reality, if the event should ever happen? I conjure gentlemen — whether from the south or the north — by all they hold dear in this world — by all their love of liberty — by all their veneration for their ancestors — by all their regard for posterity — by all their gratitude to Him who has bestowed upon them such unnumbered blessings — by all their duties which they owe to mankind, and all the duties they owe to themselves — by all these considerations, I implore them to pause, solemnly to pause — at the edge of the precipice before the fearful and disastrous leap is taken in the yawning abyss below, which will inevitably lead to certain and irretrievable destruction.

And finally, Mr. President, I implore as the best blessing which heaven can bestow upon me on earth, that if the direful and sad event of the dissolution of the union should happen, I may not survive to behold the sad and heartrending spectacle.

In cold type this is effective; what must it have been in warm impassioned speech, with the orator's eyes flashing, his matchless voice ringing out, and his whole being transformed, lofty, commanding, inspired?

It is always profitable to have a contemporary's appraisal of a famed orator. Only those who heard the man in the heyday of his power can describe for future generations the emotions stirred by a great speaker who has long since passed from the public stage. Thus Edward G. Parker, who lived in the golden days of oratory, describes Clay in action:

His manner in delivery was eminently *natural*. There was nothing artificial about it; nothing which at first rather shocked you, but which, when you got used to it, pleased you, as was the case of Mr. Pinckney's studied and splendid harangues before the Supreme Court. It was natural, easy, graceful and dignified. He never seemed, as some ranters do, to be *blowing* himself up. He never seemed to be *trying* to do anything. It was as if he couldn't help it. He was so natural and appropriate in delivery that in his wildest outbursts nobody would ever think of crying out to him, as the boy in the crowd bawled to the fuming spouter on the stage, " Sir, your face is so red, it makes me hot." No, if Clay was furious, you felt that he ought to be furious, and you would as soon find fault with a caged panther for howling as to condemn him for his outbreaks. His usual delivery was quite deliberate; every word golden and clean-cut. His hands played all ways naturally; there were no gestures which looked as if he had thought of it overnight. His figure inclined pliantly with a dignified and courtly emphasis; although in moments of vast passion it would bend almost double, and for an instant play up and down like the walking beam of a North river steamboat. His eye usually smiled with an expression of inviting good humor, alternating, however, with an expression, at times, like a jet of flame. He frequently took snuff and would walk some distance, while speaking, to take a pinch from some friendly senator's box. Sometimes he held in his hands a great red handkerchief (a product of some Kentucky loom, we should think), and often forgetting to put it in his pocket, in his rising raptures that red bandanna would flourish about with a sort of jubilant triumph of motion, breathing by the spirit of its movement as much confidence into his followers as the white plume of Henry of Navarre inspired in his soldiers. . . . Single words and tones, however, he would sometimes give with great variety of modulation; for his voice was not only full and wide-ranging, but it was under the most exact command; from his low and sweet level of tone he would sometimes strike instantly a tone like an alarm bell. We remember once hearing him *throw off* the simple words " railroad speed " in such a manner that, in an instant, he made the whole express train, under lightning headway, dash across our mind. He had too, a faculty of crowding, as by some hydrostatic pressure of oratory, an amazing weight of expression on to the backbone of a single word. Sometimes mounting from his easy level, on one word alone, he would go through a whole pantomime of action; his form rises, his eye burns, his look strikes awe, while the final ejaculation of that much anticipated word would burn it into the very fiber of the brain, for an ever-lasting memory. In boyhood, we heard him thus utter the word " crevasse "; we didn't even then know what a " crevasse " was, but it was struck, as by some tremendous die, into our mind; and has been there ever since, the type and synonym of everything appalling.

On the stump Henry Clay was irresistible. The following incident came to me by way of the great-grandson of a Whig who was present when it occurred and delighted for the rest of his life in relating the story to his friends and acquaintances.

Senator Clay and his colleague Senator J. J. Crittenden were on a speaking tour in Indiana. Arriving at Columbus late in the afternoon the two statesmen went to a tavern run by Dr. Hinman, a Democrat. Clay was feeling miserable, and at once lay down for a much needed rest. When the hour came for the big meeting Clay was so indisposed that he begged Crittenden to speak in his stead. Crittenden was aghast.

" Great God! " cried Crittenden. " Do you know what you are saying? They don't wish to hear me. They are here from all over Indiana to hear you, Clay. You must speak to these people."

" Must? " Clay looked at Crittenden quizzically. " No, I am simply through for today. There, my friend, I implore you, go on, explain my condition;

don't forget you are yourself an orator." Clay lay down again.

"All right, I'll do what I can," replied Crittenden, resignedly. "But I don't relish the job. Take a stiff drink of rock and rye and try to get some sleep."

In the parlor of the tavern Crittenden joined a small committee waiting to escort Clay and himself to the courthouse, made the necessary explanation, and with the crestfallen committee proceeded through a mass of shouting humanity to the courthouse, where with difficulty he reached the judges' stand. Turning to the throng that jammed the room Senator Crittenden called for order. Thinking he was about to introduce Clay, who they surmised was somewhere in the building, they quieted down instantly.

"Fellow Whigs," he said, "I am distressed to tell you that Senator Clay is indisposed and is in bed at the Hinman House; so, much as I know your disappointment, I will discuss with you the issues of the hour. I —"

He was interrupted by cries of "Clay!" "Henry Clay!" "Harry of the West!" "We want to hear Clay!"

"But, fellow Whigs —" Crittenden got no further. "Clay!" "Get Henry Clay out of that Democratic hotel!" "Go get Clay — get him now!" "Hurrah for Clay!"

A little nettled, Crittenden raised his voice above the storm. "All right, I'll see what I can do, but don't be disappointed if I am obliged to return without him."

Partly pacified, the crowd settled down to wait, and Crittenden returned to the tavern where he found Clay resting comfortably.

" No use, Clay, it's just as I expected; they won't listen to me. They've sent me back for you, and you have got to show yourself and say a few words. I'm sorry, but there's nothing else to do."

Clay got up and proceeded to dress, stopping to cough every few minutes. "You see, John, I'm in no fix to speak," he explained. " I'll let them hear me cough, say a few words, cough some more, and then return and leave you with the audience more than glad to listen to you."

Crittenden, suppressing a smile, managed to look solicitous, but ventured no reply. Adjusting his stock and smoothing his hair, Clay threw a cape over his shoulders, fastened it at the neck, and put on his high hat. " Give me your arm, John," he said, and leaning heavily on Crittenden he crossed the square and entered the courtroom amid wild cheering. Mounting the platform to the judges' stand, Clay stood, shoulders stooped, his face stern. The cheering was tumultuous, but at last there was quiet.

" Fellow Whigs," Clay began (a spell of coughing), " I regret I am in no condition to speak to you to-night " (another violent attack of coughing). " As you see, I am anything but a well man " (a spasm of coughing). " I — "

" Hurrah for Andy Jackson! " — the yell came from a window where lodged the one lone Democrat who had managed to get into that Whig meeting. A little groggy with drink, he balanced himself precariously. There were confusion and cries of " Throw him out! " " Sit on that Democrat! " " Throw him through the window! "

" Let that man alone; I have something I want him to hear." Clay's voice was clarion. He stood erect, his eyes flashing. He unfastened the cape and with a sweeping gesture flung it from him. " Fellow Whigs! " he thundered. " And you, my Democratic friend! Listen! I suppose when Rome was burning and Nero fiddled on, all unconcerned, some drunken Democrat shouted, ' Hurrah for Nero! ' " (Great cheering and laughter.) " And now I propose to analyze Democratic doctrine and contrast it with the clear and essentially American Whig doctrine. My fellow citizéns, the Whigs of 1842 stand where the Republicans of 1798 stood, and where the Whigs of the Revolution were battling for liberty, for the people, for free institutions, against power, against corruption, against executive encroachment, against monarchy " — and so on and on, for an hour and twenty-five minutes, with not a single cough to disturb the eloquence, the flow of perfectly balanced sentences, varied by an occasional anecdote and closing with a solemn and beautiful tribute to the flag and national unity.

It was nearly eleven o'clock when the two statesmen got to their rooms, considerably the worse for the gauntlet of handshaking they had been compelled to run. Yet both were in fine spirits. " Clay," chided Crittenden, " I thought you were indisposed; and tell me, what became of your cough? "

Clay laughed heartily. " John, I owe that drunken Democrat something. I was feeling bad, but when that fellow hurrahed for Andy Jackson I forgot my in-disposition, forgot the cough, forgot everything except the speech; why, that speech came to me as manna from heaven."

" You mean it came to the audience as manna from Clay," corrected Crittenden.

It was fated that Andrew Jackson and Clay should be adversaries, bitter political enemies, aggressive lead-ers of diverse groups. They fought nearly thirty years of fierce combat, neither asking nor giving quarter. Clay got the plaudits and Jackson got a majority of votes. Three times " Harry of the West," as Clay was affectionately called, aspired to the presidency, and as many times he went down to defeat, the third time by a narrow margin, beaten by James Knox Polk. The disappointment of Clay's friends following his third failure to grasp the grand prize was pathetic. They wept and overwhelmed him with messages of affection. Defeat seemed never to lessen his popularity.

Jackson and Clay fought fearlessly, each in his own way. When Jackson took a position he held to it stub-bornly to the end. Clay shifted his positions, made concessions, was on both sides of at least two major issues, became known as the great pacificator. One of his biographers, Joseph M. Rogers, says, " Clay's idea was that the best way to get rid of a wound was to poultice it instead of allowing it to kill or cure in the ancient barbaric fashion."

General Jackson was volcanic in wrath when fully

aroused. "Every friend was an equal, every foe a hound." And he was slow to forgive. Clay's anger was terrible for the time, but he forgave readily, bore no grudges, and soon was on good terms with himself and the world.

In the long bitter conflict between these two powerful warriors Jackson stood nearer the masses. Clay's supporters were drawn heavily from the well-to-do and the cultured. The rich and powerful were his friends. Clay dominated the Senate; Jackson ruled the people. Yet these rivals had much more in common than might appear to a casual student of their careers. Both were kind, gracious and generous to their friends; bitter, defiant and relentless toward their foes. In the words of a contemporary, " Neither could brook a rival or opposition, and each had the imperial spirit of a conqueror not to be subdued, and the pride of a leadership which could not follow." Both were the soul of gallantry toward women. Both loved and honored their country, gloried in her traditions, and served her interests, as they saw them, with signal fidelity. In the family circle they were chivalrous, warm and affectionate, touched to tears by pain and suffering. Their country homes — " The Hermitage," near Nashville, and " Ashland," on the outskirts of Lexington — were models of hospitality, where the humblest as well as the most famous guest was welcomed with Old World charm and courtesy. The pity of it is that these two high hearts were destined to be foes instead of friends.

It is not easy to cite a fair specimen of Clay's oratory, for nothing he said reads as well in type as it sounded when he delivered it to an entranced audience. However, as a rare statement of sound American policy and simple yet convincing eloquence, take his speech to Louis Kossuth. That Hungarian patriot wished the United States to come to the aid of his cause by such action as would involve the nation in the politics of Europe and might result in war. Kossuth came to Clay's hotel, accompanied by a group of distinguished friends and allies. After the usual introductions and felicitations, Clay, who was in failing health, addressed Kossuth:

I trust you will believe me, too, when I tell you that I entertain the liveliest sympathies in every struggle for liberty in Hungary, and in every country; and in this I believe I express the universal sentiment of my countrymen. But, sir, for the sake of my country, you must allow me to protest against the policy you propose to her. Waiving the grave and momentous question of the right of one nation to assume the executive power among nations for the enforcement of international law, or of the right of the United States to dictate to Russia the character of her relations with the nations around her, let us come at once to the practical consideration of the matter. . . .

The indomitable spirit of our people might and would be equal to the emergency, and we might remain unsubdued even by so tremendous a combination; but the consequences to us would be terrible enough. You must allow me, sir, to speak thus freely, as I feel deeply, though my opinion may be of but little import, as the expression of a dying man. Sir, the recent melancholy subversion of the republican government of France, and that enlightened nation voluntarily placing its neck under the yoke of despotism, teach us to despair of any present success for liberal institutions in Europe. They give us an impressive warning not to rely upon others for the vindication of our principles, but to look to ourselves, and to cherish with more care than ever the security of our institutions and the preservation of our policy and principles.

By the policy to which we have adhered since the days of Washington, we have prospered beyond precedent — we have done more for the cause of liberty in the world than arms could effect. We have showed to other nations the way to greatness and happiness; and, if we but continue united as one people, and persevere in the policy which our experience has so clearly and triumphantly vindicated, we may in another quarter of a century furnish an example which the reason of the world cannot resist. But if we should involve ourselves in the tangled web of European politics, in a war in which we could effect nothing, and if in that struggle Hungary should go down, and we should go down with her, where, then, would be the last hope of the friends of freedom throughout the world? Far better is it for ourselves, for Hungary, and for the cause of liberty, that, adhering to our wise, pacific system, and avoiding the distant wars of Europe, we should keep our lamp burning brightly on this western shore as a light to all nations, than to hazard its utter extinction amid the ruins of fallen or falling republics in Europe.

The date of this speech was December, 1851, but the wise and prudent counsel it contains is as applicable today as when it was spoken.

Before he passed from the arresting scene in which he had played so grand a part, Henry Clay made a list of the acts by which he wished to be remembered. There are fourteen items on the roll: " Senate 1806; Speaker 1811; War of 1812 with Great Britain; Ghent 1814; Missouri Compromise 1821; Spanish America 1822; American System 1824; Greece 1824; Secretary of State 1825; Panama instructions 1826; Tariff compromise 1833; Public Domain 1833–41; Peace with

ing eloquence, to which his whole manner gave ten-
fold force. When I came out I was almost afraid to
come near him. It seemed to me as if he was like the
mount that might not be touched and that burned
with fire. I was beside myself, and am so still."

The Bunker Hill oration of 1825 was another triumph. The aged General Lafayette was present and
twenty thousand people milled about the platform
where he with the other honored guests was seated.
Some of the temporary seats gave way and there was
high confusion and disorder. "It is impossible to re-
store order," said one of the committee. "Nothing is
impossible!" thundered Webster; and with lowering
brow, advancing to the front of the platform, he called
to the marshals in stentorian tones: "Let it be done.
Be silent yourselves and the people will obey." And
they did obey. It was as if he said, "Let there be
light," and there was light. The commotion ceased
and the orator, himself the son of a revolutionary vet-
eran, brought before that sea of faces a panorama of
what had happened there on the seventeenth of June,
1775. Forty survivors of the Revolution were present
to hear Webster say: "Venerable men, you have come
down to us from a former generation; . . . veterans,
you are a remnant of many a well fought field. . . .
You hear now no roar of hostile cannon, you see no
mixed volumes of smoke and flame rising from burning
Charlestown; . . . all is peace; and God has granted
you this sight of your country's happiness ere you slum-
ber in the grave forever."

Some of Webster's best oratory is unknown to the

general public. The following excerpt, for example,
from a speech delivered upon the occasion of his being charged by the Honorable Charles J. Ingersoll of
Pennsylvania with lukewarm patriotism and corruption of the party press in Maine, is worth quoting:

Sir, I grow weary, weary with this speech. Who should al-
lude to representations and imputations apparently so ground-
less? Why, sir, there is one thing in the speech from which I
will supplicate its author to have me excused. He says he never
agreed with me in politics. That is true. We never did and I
think we never shall agree. He said, many years ago, that if he
had lived in the time of the Revolution he would have been a
Tory. I don't think I would. He has said also very recently,
in a printed book of his, that the Declaration of Independence
was carried with difficulty, if not by accident. That is his esti-
mate of the great charter of our national existence. We would
never agree in politics, I admit. But he said Mr. Webster is a
man of talents. Here I beg to be excused. I can bear his abuse,
but if he undertakes my commendation, I begin to tremble for
my reputation. I ask again, what can account for the apparent
maliciousness of his statements? I do not think that they were
made through malice — I am inclined to think it proceeds from
a moral obtuseness — a native want of perception between truth
and falsehood, or the result of so long a discipline in that sublime school of morals that teaches all is fair in politics; and if
he ever possessed an iota of original, native discrimination, it is
altogether obliterated. But what does he say further? Speaking of the Treaty of Washington, he says, "the good old Bay
State," etc. He loves the old Bay State. *He* loves Massachusetts! — *He!* — *HE!* If he loves Massachusetts, he is like
    . . . That luckless swain, who grieved
    For friendship unreturned, and unrequited love.
    I can tell him, sir, the whole people of Massachusetts hold
him and his love, his principles, his speeches, his veracity, and
his value of truth in utter — what shall I say? — in anything but

respect. I don't know their motives. I say the mind of the man seems to be grotesque — *bizarre*. Why, it is rather the caricature of a mind than a mind itself. Sir, we sometimes use a phrase borrowed from mechanics; when we see a man of some knowledge and a little talent, who is found absolutely incapable of producing anything useful, we say, " There is a screw loose somewhere." In this case the screws are loose all over. The whole machine is rickety, disjointed and creaking — as often upside down as upside up; as often injurious to those who use it as doing injury to others. . . . Sir, I leave the author of these slanders where he is — I leave him in the worst company I know of in the world — I leave him with himself.

Unquestionably, Daniel Webster's greatest speech was that which he delivered in the winter of 1830, known as " The Reply to Hayne." Senator Lodge said of this speech that Webster never again surpassed or equaled it. The debate was on what was known as the Foote resolution. Senator Hayne of South Carolina, a very able and eloquent man, in a speech of marked strength and beauty had set forth the doctrine of nullification, by which was meant the right of a state to arrest the operation of a law of Congress provided the state in convention should decide that the law was unconstitutional. When young Colonel Hayne (he was only thirty-eight) had completed his speech, it seemed unanswerable. The New England senators believed their cause was lost. There was only one man in the Senate capable of making a reply, and that was Daniel Webster. The stage was set to the great orator's liking. The Senate chamber was thronged. All Washington was agog. The godlike Daniel slowly arose to face a hushed Senate. He had put on the familiar blue coat with

IV

EDWARD EVERETT

THERE IS a distinction between oratory and rhetoric. While they are closely related, indeed often interwoven, yet the distinction is there. The orator employs speech as a vehicle to convince and persuade his hearers to accept a cause or adopt a program. Thus with the orator speech is a means to an end, never the end itself. The rhetorician is largely concerned with speech as an end, often unconsciously it is true; he is enamored of the witchery of words, phrases, style. His speech is more often exhibitory than argumentative; entertaining and artistic, not primarily designed to move his audience to conviction or action. Beauty is uppermost in the mind of the rhetorician; power to move, in the mind of the orator. A great natural orator need not be a rhetorician, while a trained rhetorician may so perfect his style as to achieve oratorical triumph. In a few great public speakers the orator and rhetorician are so nicely balanced as to blend the distinction into a marvelous unity. This was true of Henry Ward Beecher, Wendell Phillips and Robert G. Ingersoll.

This preliminary observation is by way of introducing one of the most accomplished orator-rhetoricians America has produced, Edward Everett of Massachu-

setts. Born in 1794, he was educated at Harvard, and
in his twentieth year was attracting vast audiences as
a Unitarian preacher. He married into a wealthy
family, taught rhetoric at Harvard, went to Congress
for the decade 1825–35, was governor of Massachusetts,
served as minister to Great Britain, was president of
Harvard College for three years, succeeded Daniel
Webster as secretary of state in Millard Fillmore's
Cabinet, and sat in the United States Senate for a brief
period. Notable as were his public services, Everett's
career as a finished orator-rhetorician outshone every
other activity of this polished gentleman. An intimate
friend of Daniel Webster, and one of his literary ex-
ecutors, he spoke oftener than Webster; and if he
never equaled his fellow orator's greatest speeches, he
surpassed him in graceful, scholarly addresses of a cele-
brative, historic and academic character. He was an
accomplished Greek scholar, an authority on international law, and a poet whose verses held a classic flavor.
One of his famous orations was on Washington. He
delivered it throughout the country for the benefit of
the Mount Vernon Association Fund, earning a hundred thousand dollars to perpetuate that estate as a
memorial — to which fund, let it be chronicled, he
himself contributed a like sum.

If a single passage from Everett's eulogy on Washington is a fair specimen of the whole, the paragraph
which follows should be studied. It seems cold, stilted
and artificial in type, but put back of it a melodious
voice, perfect elocution, and a graceful form, and something of the effect it must have made upon the vast
audiences that listened enthralled may be regained:

Let us make a national festival and holiday of his birthday; and ever as the twenty-second of February returns, let us remember that, while with these solemn and joyous rites of observance we celebrate the great anniversary, our fellow citizens on the Hudson, on the Potomac, from the southern plains to the western lakes, are engaged in the same offices of gratitude and love. Nor we nor they alone: beyond the Ohio, beyond the Mississippi, along that stupendous trail of immigration from the east to the west, which bursting into states, as it moves westward, is already threading the western prairies, swarming through the portals of the Rocky mountains, and winding down their slopes, the name and memory of Washington on that gracious night will travel with the silver queen of heaven through sixty degrees of longitude, nor part company with her till she walks in her brightness through the Golden Gate of California, and passes serenely on to hold midnight court with the Australian stars. There and there only in barbarous archipelagoes, as yet untrodden by civilized man, the name of Washington is unknown, and there too, when they swarm with enlightened millions, new honors shall be paid with ours to his memory.

As with everything else, styles in oratory change. Where is there today a public speaker who indulges in such long, involved sentences, or dares to play with such richly embroidered imagery? Contrast this stately phrasing with Lincoln's best known utterances! The one is an exotic jungle; the other a broad and sunlit meadow. But it would be erroneous to conclude that the man who so smothered the " Father of his Country " in the flowers of speech was not able, sincere and justly famed.

Edward Everett's oratorical style was classic, cultured, sumptuous, the glorification of grace and literary excellence. Lacking Webster's majestic presence, he was even more elegant, and his voice, while not so organ-toned, was as liquid as the notes of a bird, sweet and beguiling. When he took the platform you saw a thoroughbred gentleman, self-possessed, impeccably attired, and appearing to know exactly what to do with himself and with his arms and legs. He began in a quiet manner, as one engaged in well-bred conversation in a large drawing room. Gradually he increased the volume of his voice, his gestures synchronizing with his thought to a nicety. For the most part he stood still, his voice steadily gaining power, the while pouring forth paragraphs of exquisite beauty interwoven with vivid passages of description replete with poetical effusions, and culminating in a brilliant climax that left his hearers spellbound. It was his habit to memorize his orations word for word, yet it is not recorded that he ever experienced a failure of memory or gave out a shoddy sentence on the platform. His speech was as perfect as is possible for a master of his art to achieve. There was little or no passion, no homely illustrations, but charm, beauty, artistry always — and often the tenderest pathos. This pathetic touch, so compelling, was in evidence as he concluded his Faneuil Hall oration on the death of Daniel Webster, when at the end of a superb passage he repeated these touching lines:

> His suffering ended with the day,
> Yet lived he at its close
> And breathed the long, long night away
> In statue-like repose.

But ere the sun, in all its state,
Illumed the eastern skies,
He passed through Glory's morning gate
And walked in Paradise.

One who was present on that memorable occasion has left this testimony: " As Mr. Everett uttered this peroration of poetry, we seemed to see the great man's deathbed; and as the final word ' Paradise ' stole softly and sweetly from his lips, and his form, eye, and hand reached forward gently, but apparently far upward and onward to the sky, we could almost feel as if we were there ourselves, for one instant vanishing from earth with him, and going hand in hand with that great shade up to that ' morning gate.' "

By general consent of his contemporaries, Everett's most effective oration was his Phi Beta Kappa address at Harvard in 1824, when Lafayette was present. Usually this polished rhetorician held himself in leash, but that day he let himself go in an emotional outburst of resplendent eloquence. One who was present pronounced Everett's apostrophe to Lafayette " a splendid conflagration." Here is the famous passage — slightly abbreviated — the passage that was so overpowering that, to quote one present, " every man in the assembly was in tears." At an appropriate moment Everett turned to General Lafayette, then an old man and about to say farewell to America forever:

Welcome, friend of our fathers, to our shores! Happy are our eyes that behold those venerable features! Enjoy a triumph such as never conqueror or monarch enjoyed — the assurance that throughout America there is not a bosom which does not beat with joy and gratitude at the sound of your name. . . . But you have looked in vain for the faces of many who would have lived years of pleasure on a day like this, with their old companion in arms and brother in peril. . . . Above all, the first of heroes and of men, the friend of your youth, the more than friend of his country, rests in the bosom of the soil he redeemed. On the banks of his Potomac he lies in glory and in peace. You will revisit the hospitable shades of Mount Vernon; but him whom you venerated as we did you will not meet at its door. His voice of consolation, which reached you in the Austrian dungeons, cannot now break its silence, to bid you welcome to his own roof. But the grateful children of America will bid you welcome in his name. Welcome! thrice welcome to our shores! And whithersoever throughout the limits of the continent your course shall take you, the ear that hears you shall bless you, the eye that sees you shall bear witness to you, and every tongue exclaim with heartfelt joy, Welcome! Welcome! Lafayette!

On July 4, 1828, Everett was the orator of the day at Charlestown, where he spoke on " The History of Liberty." The oration he delivered that day is an example of Everett at his best. He delighted in historical discourses; he was peculiarly at home with such a theme. There follows one of his finest passages:

You need not, friends and fellow citizens, that I should dwell upon the incidents of the last great acts in the colonial drama. This very place was the scene of some of the earliest and the most memorable of them, and their recollection is a part of your inheritance of honor. In the early councils and first struggles of the great revolutionary enterprise, the citizens of this place were among the most prominent. The measures of resistance which were projected by the patriots of Charlestown were opposed by but one individual. An active cooperation existed between the political leaders in Boston and this place. The beacon light which was kindled in the towers of Christ Church in Boston, on the night of the eighteenth of April, 1775, was answered from the steeple of the church in which we are now assembled. The intrepid messenger who was sent forward to convey to Hancock and Adams the intelligence of the approach of the British troops was furnished with a horse, for his eventful errand, by a respected citizen of this place. At the close of the following momentous day, the British forces — the remnant of its disasters — found refuge, under the shades of night, upon the heights of Charlestown; and there, on the ever memorable seventeenth of June, that great and costly sacrifice in the cause of freedom was consummated with fire and blood. Your hilltops were strewed with illustrious dead; your homes were wrapped in flames; the fair fruits of a century and a half of civilized culture were reduced to a heap of bloody ashes, and two thousand men, women and children turned houseless on the world. With the exception of the ravages of the nineteenth of April, the chalice of woe and desolation was in this manner first presented to the lips of the citizens of Charlestown. Thus devoted, as it were, to the cause, it is no wonder that the spirit of the Revolution should have taken possession of their bosoms, and been transmitted to their children. The American who, in any part of the union, could forget the scenes and the principles of the Revolution, would thereby prove himself unworthy of the blessings which he enjoys; but the citizen of Charlestown who could be cold on this momentous theme must hear a voice of reproach from the walls which were reared on the ashes of the seventeenth of June — a piercing cry from the very sods of yonder hill.

It might be thought that this widely traveled scholarbookman would not need to slave over his speeches, devote weeks to the composition of an address, rewrite a single paragraph a score of times; yet this prince of rhetoricians followed just such a course. He invariably made the most exacting preparation, and when the

hour came for the delivery of the oration he was letter
perfect. Edward G. Parker, a contemporary, thus
comments at length on this aspect of Everett's character:

Everett, so far from seeking to conceal his ample preparation, is very properly proud of it. And how much it reflects
upon the arrogance of youth, which too often airs its audacious
conceits " on the spur of the moment " before audiences to
whom Edward Everett, at the age of sixty, thinks himself un-
equal to speak without learned and practiced labors! We remember hearing how, in a political campaign a few years ago,
he astonished a Boston Young Men's Committee by this trait.
They came to him about a fortnight beforehand with a respect-
ful request that he address a great Faneuil Hall caucus. " Why,
gentlemen," said the monarch of the platform, " you only give
me two weeks to prepare! " And he declined the invitation;
only " two weeks to prepare "! And the orator who said so was
at the time a man of absolute leisure; a leisure almost Otto-
manic in the profound security of a secluded and splendid library.

It may, however, be thrown in as a slight qualification of
the inference to be drawn from Everett's thorough and exquisite detail of preparation, that the whole temper of his
genius is literary and studious. We doubt if he COULD speak
extempore, if he would. Addison, secretary of state for England, was nevertheless powerless to tell the world his thought,
or indeed to tell it to himself, till he got a pen in his fingers;
and perhaps it is equally so with Everett, secretary of state for
America. He has certainly " the dash of ink in his blood."
White paper and black marks are the wadding and powder of
all his intellectual volleys. He is all over, a bookman. At
Harvard University, where they all copy him; and where their
annually renewing homage seems to float incense to him as
from an ever burning altar with the name of " Everett " upon
it — there the Alma Mater still fondly recalls that brilliant boy

who was fitted for college at nine years of age, and entered her learned precincts at thirteen, to run the round of academic glories with a splendid ardor, like Phaeton wheeling the golden chariot, but without A FALL.

Everett had his critics, and still has them. Phillip Russell, in his *Emerson, the Wisest American,* has a paragraph with a sting in its tail. "The flowers of oratorical rhetoric were admired no less by Harvard boys than by their parents," writes Russell, "and the chief matinee idol of the faculty was Edward Everett, professor of Greek literature. To prepare himself for this chair Everett had visited Europe. From there he returned laden with metaphors, curios and similes, which he flung to his audiences as if they were violets. On the platform he did not so much speak as prance. He had gifts as an actor which he spread lavishly before his entranced students. Emerson admired him extravagantly until he discovered that his carefully posed idol had feet of clay which vainly tried to look like Daniel Webster's."

In September, 1863, plans were made to dedicate the cemetery at Gettysburg, and the date was set for October 23. An invitation was issued to Edward Everett, the foremost orator of that day, to deliver the address. He replied it would be impossible for him to make adequate preparation at the time proposed, so to meet his convenience dedication was postponed nearly a month, until Thursday, November 19. Later, and almost as an afterthought, the President of the United States was asked to make "a few appropriate remarks." The great day dawned bright, clear, warm and pleasant. There was a procession, bands of music played, banners streamed, flags were flung to the breeze, and twenty thousand people thronged the little Pennsylvania town. Everett had made extensive preparation; he had written his speech out in full, committed it, and very likely rehearsed it. Leaving nothing to chance, he had spent three days in Gettysburg and thoroughly studied the field. He made use of reports supplied by General Meade, and he knew by heart every move, skirmish, charge of the three days' battle. White-haired and erect, in his seventieth year, fully aware of the importance of the occasion, Edward Everett was introduced and looked about him. On the platform was President Lincoln along with other celebrities. In front of him a vast throng, hushed into silence by the sad memories. Nearby were the newly made graves of thousands who but a few months before were in the glow and beauty of life. Touched by the surroundings, Everett extemporized this opening paragraph:

Standing beneath this serene sky, overlooking these broad fields, now reposing from the waning year, the mighty Alleghenies dimly towering before us, the graves of our brethren beneath our feet, it is with hesitation that I raise my poor voice to break the eloquent silence of God and nature. But the duty to which you have called me must be performed — grant me, I pray you, your indulgence and sympathy.

These words disclose a becoming spirit, truly humble and fundamentally noble. Without manuscript or even a note, Everett spoke for an hour and fifty-seven minutes, a notable speech, sparkling with classical allusions, heavy with a mass of detailed references to the three days' engagements, relieved here and there by vivid descriptive passages that must have been most effective in their delivery. The speech was not wholly free from the note of bitterness, but we must remember that the terrible war was in progress and only the Christlike can forgive enemies. The peroration is too long to quote in its entirety, but here is a section of the final paragraph:

God bless the union; it is dearer to us for the blood of the brave men shed in its defense. The spots on which they stood and fell; these pleasant heights; the fertile plain beneath them; the thriving village whose streets so lately rang with the strange din of war; the fields beyond the ridge, where the noble Reynolds held the advancing foe at bay, and while he gave up his own life, assured by his forethought and self-sacrifice the triumph of the two succeeding days; the little streams which wind through the hills, on whose banks in aftertimes the wondering ploughman will turn up, with the rude weapons of savage warfare, the fearful missiles of modern artillery; the Seminary ridge, the peach orchard, cemetery, Culp's and Wolf's hills, Round Top, Little Round Top, humble names, henceforward dear and famous; no lapse of time, no distance of space shall cause you to be forgotten . . . wheresoever throughout the civilized world the accounts of this great warfare are read, and down to the latest period of recorded time, in the glorious annals of our common country, there will be no brighter page than that which relates THE BATTLES OF GETTYSBURG.

There was another speech that day. It followed Edward Everett's, and it was shorter than many of that orator's paragraphs; and this speech — but that is another story!

WENDELL PHILLIPS

The Amphionic Agitator

V

WENDELL PHILLIPS

ON THE AFTERNOON of October 21, 1835, in the city of Boston, a young lawyer sat beside an open window in his office on Court street reading. Suddenly his attention was attracted by a shouting and a tumult and the tramp of many feet beneath his window. The young lawyer arose and leaned over the window sill; half a block away he saw a crowd apparently under great excitement. He put on his hat, went out into the street, and found himself in the midst of a mob. A man, bareheaded, with a rope about his waist, his clothing torn, but with erect head and calm face, was being dragged toward the city hall. Cries of " Kill him! " " Lynch him! " " Hang the fellow! " filled the air. "Who is that?" the young attorney asked of a bystander. " *That*," was the answer, " why, that's William Lloyd Garrison, the damned abolitionist; they're going to hang him." The youthful lawyer, seeing the commander of the Boston regiment, of which he was himself a member, approached him and said, " Colonel, why doesn't the mayor call out the regiment?" " Why," retorted the officer, " don't you see that the regiment is in the mob? " The young lawyer scrutinized the throng about him. Yes, it was true, it was a mob in broadcloth. He turned and walked back to his office in deep thought. That very day the young lawyer, Wendell Phillips, made a momentous decision whereby the aristocracy of Boston lost one of its proudest sons and the abolition cause won a convert.

Born of fine old New England stock, carefully educated at the Boston Latin School, a graduate of Harvard College and the Harvard Law School, a patrician in appearance, speech and spirit, Phillips was remarkable for his tantalizing eloquence and for a character of singular purity. When he was a boy of fourteen he heard quaint, forthright Lyman Beecher preach on the theme, "You Belong to God," and of this episode he said: "I went home after the service, threw myself on the floor in my room, with locked doors, and prayed, 'O God, I belong to Thee, take what is Thine own'; I asked this, that whenever a thing be wrong, it may have no power of temptation over me; whenever a thing be right, it may take no courage to do it. From that day to this it has been so." I quote this statement of Phillips' believing it to be the secret of his stormy but fruitful career.

When Boston's bluebloods learned that Wendell Phillips had become an abolitionist they were petrified with amazement and chagrin. His family in all its branches felt disgraced; former classmates stood aghast; Beacon Hill rent its garments and put ashes on its head. The Back Bay colony and the elite of Cambridge said of Phillips' decision, "It is suicide, political, professional and social suicide." So it was. Old acquaintances cut him dead. Doors which had once opened to give him hospitable welcome were shut in his face. He found himself an outcast in his native city. He had become a member of that despised group of agitators with the fiery Garrison at their head and a troop of wild-eyed fanatics trailing behind. Wendell Phillips' dreams of success at the bar, visions of succeeding Webster and Everett in the Senate, of a high diplomatic or Cabinet position, dissolved like fantastic bubbles in the air. He was a social Benedict Arnold in the city of his birth. The die was cast. For the rest of his life he gave himself, first to the cause of the slave, continuing that fight until the thirteenth amendment was written into the Constitution. Then he supported labor, woman's suffrage, opposition to capital punishment, temperance reform, and the cause of Irish freedom. Ever the agitator, his pellucid eloquence and uncommon gifts of mind made him one of the lords of the lyceum in the great old days when Henry Ward Beecher, John B. Gough, Edward Everett, and other princes of the platform spoke to the delight of multitudes.

The oratory of Wendell Phillips is unlike that of the other great speakers of that golden age of oratory. His was the oratory both of light and of white heat. He loved the short tingling sentence that slices like a saber. He was never platitudinous or trite. His delivery was surprisingly quiet, so that one hearing him for the first time would say, "Can this be the famed Wendell Phillips of whom I have heard so much?" For the larger part, his style was conversational, the tone colloquial and cool, yet it was the raciest style, in the sense of piquancy and brilliant epigrammatic quality, the nation has known. He was the orator of radicalism. He said daring things in dulcet tones. There are public speakers who stamp their feet, clench their fists, fight the air, and bellow like a bull, yet what they say is harmless and commonplace. Phillips exploded verbal bombs in the calmest fashion. He torpedoed long-accepted customs as serenely and matter-of-factly as one might say, " Be so kind as to pass the butter." Listen to some of his epigrams: " Peace if possible, but justice at any rate. . . ." " If the pot cannot hold the plant, let it crack. . . ." " All revolutions come from below. . . ." " The proper time to maintain one's rights is when they are denied; the proper persons to maintain them are those to whom they are denied. . . ." " Liberty even in defeat knows nothing but victory." He was a master of epithets — epithets that clung and kept their sting.

Phillips' reputation as an orator became nation-wide overnight when he took the platform in a critical moment at a meeting called December 8, 1837, at Faneuil Hall, to protest against the murder of Elijah P. Lovejoy, the abolitionist, at Alton, Illinois. The famous old hall was crowded to suffocation with antislavery proponents — abolitionists, who predominated; mobocrats bent on mischief; and a crowd of spectators attracted by curiosity. Resolutions were drawn by Dr. Channing, properly offered and seconded; immediately there was a stir while the attorney general of Massachusetts, big-voiced James T. Austin, took the platform and in tones of thunder sought to confuse the people and prevent a vote on the resolution. The attorney general was a good deal of a demagogue and played upon the prejudices of his auditors. His speech was effective. It looked as if the foes of freedom had captured the hall. It was at this moment that Wendell Phillips, who had come to the meeting with no thought of speaking, leaped upon the platform and faced the tempestuous multitude. The unexpectedness of the appearance of the handsome youth of twenty-six gained him a hearing. Very quietly he began in his marvelous voice, sweet as a song, clear as a flute:

Mr. Chairman: We have met for the freest discussion of these resolutions, and the events which gave rise to them. [Cries of " Question! " " Hear him! " " Go on! " " No gagging! " etc.] I hope I shall be permitted to express my surprise not only at such sentiments from such a man, but at the applause they have received within these walls. A comparison has been drawn between the events of the Revolution and the tragedy at Alton. We have heard it asserted here, in Faneuil Hall, that Great Britain had a right to tax the colonies, and we have heard the mob at Alton, the drunken murderers of Lovejoy, compared to those patriot fathers who threw the tea overboard! [Great applause.] Fellow citizens, is this Faneuil Hall doctrine? [" No, no."] The mob at Alton were met to wrest from a citizen his just rights — met to resist the laws. We have been told that our fathers did the same; and the glorious mantle of revolutionary precedent has been thrown over the mobs of our day. . . . To draw the conduct of our ancestors into a precedent for mobs, for a right to resist laws we ourselves have enacted, is an insult to their memory. . . . Sir, when I heard the gentleman lay down principles which place the murderers of Alton side by side with Otis and Hancock, with Quincy and Adams, I thought those pictured lips [pointing to the portraits in the hall] would have broken into voice to rebuke the recreant American — the slanderer of the dead!

" Here," says a famous account of the incident, " there were applause and hisses, with cries of ' Take that back.' The uproar became so great that for a long time no one could be heard. At length the Honorable William Sturgis came to Mr. Phillips' side at the front of the platform. He was met with mingled cries of ' Phillips or nobody! ' ' Make him take back " recreant "! ' ' He shan't go on till he takes it back! ' When it was understood that Mr. Sturgis meant to sustain, not to interrupt Mr. Phillips, he was listened to, and said, ' I entreat you, fellow citizens, . . . by every association connected with this hall, consecrated by our fathers to freedom of discussion, that you listen to every man who addresses you in a decorous manner.' Mr. Phillips resumed."

Fellow citizens, I cannot take back my words. Surely, the attorney general, so long and well known here, needs not the aid of your hisses against one so young as I am — my voice never before heard within these walls!

Then came this volcanic flame-burst:

The gentleman said he should sink into insignificance if he condescended to gainsay the principles of these resolutions. For the sentiments he has uttered on the soil consecrated by the prayers of Puritans and the blood of patriots, the earth should have yawned and swallowed him up!

Having discomfited the attorney general, he continued:

Is it *presumptuous* to assert the freedom of the press on American ground! Is the assertion of such freedom before the age? So much before the age as to leave one no right to make it because it displeases the community? It is this very thing which entitles Lovejoy to greater praise, the disputed right which provoked the Revolution — taxation without representation — is far beneath that for which he died. [Here there was a strong and general expression of disapprobation.] One word, gentlemen. As much as *thought* is better than *money*, so much is the cause in which Lovejoy died nobler than a mere question of taxes. James Otis thundered in this hall when the king did but touch his *pocket*. Imagine, if you can, his indignant eloquence had England offered to put a gag upon his *lips*. [Great applause.]

One of the most popular lyceum lectures on the American platform was Wendell Phillips' " The Lost Arts." The thesis of this composition was that there is nothing new under the sun. He delivered this lecture throughout the country, more than two thousand times, and it earned for him and the causes in which he was interested the sum of one hundred sixty-five thousand dollars. Next to Russell Conwell's famous " Acres of Diamonds " it was the most successful single lecture and the most profitable in a monetary way in the history of the American lyceum. His oration on Daniel O'Connell, delivered in Boston August 6, 1870, is a magnificent piece of stirring oratory, full of passages that even in print sparkle and coruscate. His tribute to the eloquence of O'Connell, in which he compares him to contemporary orators, is most brilliant. Consider this paragraph:

His eloquence has never been equaled in modern times, certainly not in English speech. Do you think I am partial? I will vouch John Randolph of Roanoke, the Virginian slaveholder, who hated an Irishman almost as much as he hated a Yankee,

himself an orator of no mean level. Hearing O'Connell, he
exclaimed, " This is the man, these are the lips, the most eloquent that speak English in my day." I think he was right. I
remember the solemnity of Webster, the grace of Everett, the
rhetoric of Choate; I know the eloquence that lay hid in the
iron logic of Calhoun; I have melted beneath the magnetism of
Seargent S. Prentiss of Mississippi, who wielded a power few
men ever had. It has been my fortune to sit at the feet of the
great speakers of the English tongue on the other side of the
ocean. But I think all of them together never surpassed, and
no one of them ever equaled, O'Connell. . . . I heard him
once say, " I send my voice across the Atlantic, careening like
the thunderstorm against the breeze, to tell the slaveholders of
the Carolinas that God's thunderbolts are hot, and to remind the bondman that the dawn of his redemption is already
breaking." You seemed to hear the tones come echoing back to
London from the Rocky mountains. Then, with the slightest
possible Irish brogue, he would tell a story, while all Exeter
Hall shook with laughter. The next moment, tears in his voice
like a Scotch song, five thousand men wept. And all the while
no effort. He seemed only breathing.

" As effortless as woodland nooks
    Send violets up, and paint them blue."

How great public speakers prepare their speeches is
a matter of interest to many. Some pace the floor, or
take to the woods or the city streets. Others must have
a pen in hand and think best as they write. Not a few
modern orators dictate to stenographers. Webster
composed while engaged in his favorite sport of fishing.
Clay as a young orator declaimed to livestock, cattle
and sheep, as he strolled through blue grass pastures.
Phillips stretched himself out on a couch and prepared
his speeches as he studied the ceiling. And he could
extemporize on his feet with a fluency and accuracy

that were amazing. He had a first-class mind, read constantly, and remembered dates and names with a non-
chalant ease that delighted his hearers.

In the summer of 1881, Phillips delivered the Phi
Beta Kappa oration at Harvard, speaking on the subject, " The Scholar in a Republic." It was a tardy recognition by his own college. Much was expected of
him. There was a great deal of speculation, and some
apprehension, as to what use the orator would make of
the occasion. James Freeman Clarke, a Harvard alum-
nus and an author, said that when he knew that Wendell Phillips was to give the Phi Beta Kappa oration
he was curious to know what course he would take —
that he had two opportunities, one to deliver a grand
academic discourse, and the other to rebuke Cambridge
culture for its halfhearted support of movements in behalf of the oppressed and the wronged. Dr. Clarke has
left the testimony that Phillips accepted and used both
opportunities, that he gave an oration the equal of any
of Everett's or Sumner's, and at the same time he " arraigned and condemned all scholarship as essentially
timid, selfish, and unheroic." The following excerpts
taken from this oration hold some of its sparkle and
bite:

What Wyclif did for religion, Jefferson and Sam Adams did
for the state — they trusted it to the people. He gave the masses
the Bible, the right to think. Jefferson and Sam Adams gave
them the ballot, the right to rule. His intrepid advance contemplated theirs as its natural, inevitable result. Their serene
faith completed the gift which the Anglo-Saxon race makes to
humanity. We have not only established a new measure of the

possibilities of the race; we have laid on strength, wisdom and skill a new responsibility.

Grant that each man's relations to God and his neighbor are exclusively his own concern, and that he is entitled to all the aid that will make him the best judge of these relations; that the people are the source of all power, and their measureless capacity the lever of all progress; their sense of right the court of final appeal in civil affairs; the institutions they create the only ones any power has a right to impose; that the attempt of one class to prescribe the law, the religion, the morals, or the trade of another is both unjust and harmful — and the Wyclif and Jefferson of history mean this if they mean anything — then when, in 1867, Parliament doubled the English franchise, Robert Lowe was right in affirming, amid the cheers of the House, " Now the first interest and duty of every Englishman is to educate the masses — our masters. . . ."

It is not the masses who have most disgraced our political annals. I have seen many mobs between the seaboard and the Mississippi. I never saw or heard of any but well dressed mobs, assembled and countenanced, if not always led in person, by respectability and what called itself education. That unrivaled scholar, the first and greatest New England ever lent to Congress, signaled his advent by quoting the original Greek of the New Testament in support of slavery, and offering to shoulder his musket in its defense; and forty years later the last professor who went to quicken and lift the moral mood of those halls is found advising a plain, blunt, honest witness to forge and lie, that this scholarly reputation might be saved from wreck. Singular comment on Landor's sneer that there is a spice of the scoundrel in most of our literary men. But no exacting level of property qualification for a vote would have saved those stains. In those cases Judas did not come from the unlearned class. . . .

Nihilism is the righteous and honorable resistance of a people crushed under an iron rule. Nihilism is evidence of life. When " order reigns in Warsaw," it is spiritual death. Nihilism is the last weapon of victims choked and manacled beyond all other resistance. It is crushed humanity's only means of making the oppressor tremble. God means that unjust power shall be insecure; and every move of the giant, prostrate in chains, whether it be to lift a single dagger or stir a city's revolt, is a lesson in justice. . . . I honor nihilism; since it redeems human nature from the suspicion of being utterly vile, made up only of heartless oppressors and contented slaves. . . . Chatham rejoiced when our fathers rebelled. For every single reason they alleged, Russia counts a hundred, each one ten times bitterer than any Hancock or Adams could give. Sam Johnson's standing toast in Oxford port was, " Success to the first insurrection of slaves in Jamaica," a sentiment Southey echoed. " Eschew cant," said that old moralist. But of all the cants that are canted in this canting world, though the cant of piety may be the worst, the cant of Americans bewailing Russian nihilism is the most disgusting.

Among the numerous tributes paid to Phillips after his death, that by the Negro orator Frederick Douglass is of uncommon interest, for the two men had wrought for a common cause, fighting shoulder to shoulder. Not only so, but in this tribute appears as fine an analysis of the oratory of Wendell Phillips as can anywhere be found. Douglass said:

Mr. Phillips' oratory, like the oratory of all men, had its period of youth, its middle age, and its old age. When young, his style was ornate, and abounded in word pictures. More than forty years ago when he had just returned from a tour of Europe, where he witnessed the disgraceful position this republic had been made to occupy by General Cass, our minister to France, in refusing to sign the quintuple treaty for the abolition of the slave trade, he made a speech in the Tabernacle in New York which illustrated this youthful quality of his oratory. " As I stood," he said, " on the shores of Genoa and saw our beautiful American ship the *Ohio* floating on the placid Mediterranean, with her masts tapering proportionately aloft, her pinion flying, and an eastern sun reflecting her graceful form upon the sparkling waters, attracting the gaze of the multitude on the shore, I thought the scene one to pride any American to think himself an American, but when I thought that in all probability the first time that gallant ship should gird on her gorgeous apparel and wake from beneath her sides dominant thunder, it would be in defense of the African slave trade, I could but blush and hang my head in shame."

On another occasion, after tracing the progress of liberty, under the symbol of the eagle, from Greece to Rome and from Rome to western Europe, and thence to America, he made an impressive pause in his rapid sketch, and while his audience were yet under the spell of his matchless eloquence, he exclaimed: " Did God send that eagle here to die? Did he form the Mississippi valley for its grave? Did he pile up the Rocky mountains for its monument? Did he pour out Niagara's thunder for its requiem? " This florid style of the young orator was early laid aside for a more direct and dignified one which grew more and more chaste with his advancing years.

Douglass continues: " Perfect as Mr. Phillips was as a speaker, he lacked one element of a perfect orator. He could make men think, make them angry, make them wince under his scathing denunciation; he could make them smile, but he could not bring young tears from mature eyes. His mission was to point out the defects in the thoughts, speech and actions of others; to expose the shortcomings of men — and he did this unsparingly and thoroughly." This is a keen criticism, and it helps to account for the phrase, " a brilliant scold," more than once applied to Phillips.

Wendell Phillips is one of the noblest examples in this country of natural eloquence, highly developed and under perfect control, consecrated to human betterment. It is easy to find fault with his extreme statements, criticize his caustic gift of sarcasm and invective, deprecate his vituperation; but no one could cast aspersions on his character, which was as flawless as a human being can achieve. He inherited a modest fortune and gave it away to aid the disinherited, the friendless, the poor. He earned another fortune on the platform, and dispensed it among the needy. His was a legacy of cultured lineage, a recognized place in Boston's accepted society, together with marvelous natural gifts of voice, presence, intellect, and the advantages that come with university training and wide travel — all of these he put upon the high altar of devotion to unpopular causes. He was a breaker of chains, a smasher of worn out traditions, a pioneer thinker, a clarion voice in the wilderness crying " Repent ye, repent ye! "

On the west side of the Public Gardens of Boston there is a bronze statue of Wendell Phillips. Passers-by stop to study it; tourists focus their cameras upon it. No wonder. The statue is arresting. In his left hand the figure holds broken chains — most eloquent of symbols. Under the shining name of " Liberator " this orator lives!

SEARGENT S. PRENTISS

Orator of Purple Patches

VI

SEARGENT S. PRENTISS

ONE OF THE MOST magnetic and scintillating of
the great spellbinders of a period opulent with
eloquent speakers was Seargent Smith Prentiss of Mississippi. Wendell Phillips called him " the most eloquent
of all southerners," and Daniel Webster averred that
the only man he ever heard equal a speech by Prentiss
was Prentiss himself. High praise from authoritative
sources. Contemporary records corroborate this ap-
praisement, showing that few American orators so completely mastered an audience as did Prentiss of Mississippi.

Prentiss was not a southerner by birth, but a New
Englander, born September 30, 1808, in Portland,
Maine. Through an illness in childhood he was permanently lamed and obliged to walk by the aid of a
cane the rest of his life. He was a sensitive child, highly
imaginative, and his remarkable fluency of speech was
exhibited early. There is a tradition that he made his
first stump speech in an apple orchard to a mass meeting
of playmates and that when he finished they shouted,
" Go on, go on! "

Prentiss entered Bowdoin College and his record
there was brilliant. He became adept in Latin and

Greek, and excelled in English literature, feeding liberally on Byron, Shakespeare, Scott and Milton. Yet he
was not exactly a bookworm and certainly not a recluse.
He frolicked with his friends and in those years formed
the convivial habits which strongly marked his later
career.

In 1826, at the age of eighteen, Prentiss was granted
the A. B. degree from Bowdoin and took up the study
of law. Shortly thereafter he left New England for the
west and south. After wanderings which led him
through Boston, New York, Niagara Falls, Cincinnati
and Louisville, he arrived at the place destined to be his
home and the scene of some of his notable triumphs —
Natchez, Mississippi.

The young fortune hunter landed in that lively little
city with exactly five dollars in his pocket, and the manner in which he spent his all and established himself in
the hearts of the people became one of the legends of
Natchez.*

Prentiss went to the Mansion House, à popular tavern kept by John Bell, locally renowned for something
or other. The young man from Maine walked into the
hotel office which was filled with guests and citizens
who gazed at him curiously, took a look about him and
invited the company to the bar, where he spent the five
dollars for liquor and cigars. In later years when
chided for his prodigality on this occasion, Prentiss' re-
joinder was that by this act he " established his credit "

* It may be read in a slightly different version in *The Life and Times
of Seargent S. Prentiss,* by Joseph D. Shields, a good solid volume that is
out of print and hard to find.

in the community. Perhaps he did, for the newcomer
got on from the first. He became a tutor in a home of
wealth and culture, taught in an academy, organized a
debating society in which his own gifts shone lustrously,
and made myriad friends, some of whom in later years
became eminent in business and politics. Despite his
lameness Prentiss was a dashing, handsome young fellow, much sought after, a charming conversationalist
and with something of the cavalier in his bearing and
spirit.

Two years of teaching supplied Prentiss with enough
funds to resume his law studies. He entered the office
of Robert J. Walker, afterward United States senator,
and in June 1829 was admitted to the bar. He was not
yet twenty-one and his progress in the profession was
extremely rapid. In order to facilitate his legal opportunities Prentiss moved to Vicksburg in 1832 and
opened an office there. The bar in that city was especially notable at that time, and among the leaders this
stripling took his place with ease and maintained it.

In 1837 he was elected to Congress, but not seated;
reelected at the polls he took his seat at Washington
after another bitterly fought contest. It was at a time
when the orators ruled both the House and the Senate.
Webster, Clay and Calhoun were in the zenith of their
powers, Everett in his splendid prime, Crittenden and
Menifee of Kentucky stars of the first oratorical magnitude, and among them all S. S. Prentiss not only held his
own, but won new honors and additional fame. He returned to speak in his old home at Portland and was
welcomed as a conqueror. He spoke in Boston, New

York and other cities.   He appeared jointly with Webster and Everett and won the plaudits of wildly cheering crowds.   He loved the life, but it wore and depleted
his never robust health.

The oratorical style of Seargent S. Prentiss was florid
in his earlier career, and to the end richly embroidered.
It abounded in descriptive passages of rare beauty and
was full of rhetorical surprises.   His manner was
stately, solemn and dignified if the occasion warranted,
colloquial, poetical and whimsical if the situation permitted.   More volatile even than Clay, he was not so
ponderous as Webster; less polished than Everett, he
was more impassioned.   Usually he spoke at length —
one, two, even three hours — and held his audience to
the last syllable.   As a specimen of his earlier oratory
the opening and closing paragraphs of the eulogy on the
death of Lafayette make good reading.   The year was
1834 and the orator was on the throne:

Death, who knocks with equal hand at the door of the cottage and at the palace gate, has been busy at work; mourning
prevails throughout the land, and the countenances of all are
shrouded in the mantle of regret.   Far across the wide Atlantic,
amid the pleasant vineyards on the sunny lands of France,
there, too, is mourning, and the weeds of sorrow are all there,
worn by prince and peasant.   The friend and companion of
Washington is no more!   He who taught the eagle of our country while yet unfledged to plume his young wing and mate his
talons with the lion's strength, has taken his flight far beyond
the stars, beneath whose influence he fought so well! . . . Lafayette is no more! . . .

Peace be to his ashes!   Calm and quiet may they rest upon
some vine-clad hill of his own beloved land, which should be

called the Mount Vernon of France. Let no cunning sculpture, no monumental marble, deface with its mock dignity the patriot's grave, but, rather, let the unpruned vine, the wildflower, and the free song of the uncaged bird, all that speaks of freedom and peace, be gathered around it. Lafayette needs no mausoleum, his epitaph is graved in the heart of man.

Greatly admired as this oration was, it was a carefully prepared speech and Prentiss was never quite so effective as in extempore oratory. Huge audiences inspired him, the sight and " feel " of them went to his head like beady liquor. He used to say that an audience magnetized him.

Perhaps an extract from a speech Prentiss made in Faneuil Hall at a public dinner given Daniel Webster will serve to show him at his best. Webster, ex-Governor Ellsworth and Edward Everett were on the program and the hour was very late when Prentiss was introduced. The excerpts which follow are taken from a verbatim report made at the time of delivery and include notations of the applause and cheers that punctuated them:

I return my most sincere and profound thanks for the honor that has been done to me and to the state which I have the good fortune in part to represent. I hardly know in what form to present what I have to say, or where to begin. It has been my lot, especially of late, to address my fellow citizens on various occasions and under almost all possible outward circumstances. Sometimes I have spoken to them under no other roof than the broad arch of heavens; at other times canopied by the branches of the primeval forests of the southwest; at others within the structures of the hands of man; but never have I stood before an audience in such circumstances as here surround me. Never before have I listened to the echo of my own voice from the walls of old Faneuil Hall. [Cheers.] I hardly know whether to address myself to the dim and venerable shadows of the past or the more real and palpable forms which meet my eye. Faneuil Hall may be justly styled the mecca of liberty. [Great cheering.] Ay, and the mecca of Whigism also. [Immense cheering.]

. . . .

There is another precious vital interest which is assailed with no less desperate rashness: it is our union itself. This is attempted to be destroyed by arraying the local prejudices in mutual hostility, by stirring up a sectional warfare — the north and the south, the east and the west — as though the common glory and the common interest of the whole country was not more than sufficient to outweigh a thousand times the local and minor matters in which we differ. But though politicians, actuated solely by a selfish and parricidal ambition, seek to rend asunder what God himself has joined in everlasting bonds, there is a hand that will arrest the impious design — a hand they despise, but which they will find too strong for them — I mean the hard hand of MECHANICAL LABOR! [Great cheering.] Yes, sir, that mighty hand, and long may it be might in this free and equal land — that mighty hand will link these states together with hooks of steel. The laboring population of this country mean to live together as one people, and who shall disannul their purpose? See how they are conquering time and space! See the thousand steamboats that traverse our lakes and rivers; ay, and that, leviathan-like, begin to make the ocean itself *to boil like a pot!* Look at their railroad cars glancing like fiery meteors from one end of the land to the other; blazing centaurs with untiring nerves, with unwasting strength, and who seem to go, too, on the grand *temperance* principle, laboring all day on *water* only! [Laughter and loud cheering.] Think you the American people will suffer their cars to stop, their railroads to be broken in twain, and all their majestic rivers severed or changed in their courses because these politicians choose to draw a dividing line between a northern and a southern empire? Never, sir! Never! Proceeding on those great national principles of union which have been so luminously expounded and so nobly vindicated by your illustrious guest [cheers], they will teach these politicians who is MASTER. Let us hang together for fifty years longer, and we may defy the world to separate us! [Shouts and repeated cheers.] Let us but safely get through this crisis, and our institutions will stand on a firmer basis than ever! [Cheers.]

In print this extract seems jumbled and not exceptional, but the testimony of experts is at hand. Of this speech Edward Everett wrote: " It seemed to me the most wonderful specimen of sententious fluency which I ever witnessed. The words poured from his lips in a torrent, but the sentences were correctly formed, the train of thought distinctly pursued, the matter grave and important, the illustrations wonderfully happy, drawn from a wide range of reading and aided by a brilliant imagination. Sitting by Mr. Webster, I asked him if he had ever heard anything like it. He answered, ' Never, except from Prentiss himself.' "

Wendell Phillips enjoyed relating the following incident: Once when Prentiss was defending the tariff before a crowd of four thousand people in his state, in the course of an eloquent period which rose to a beautiful climax he painted the thrift, the energy, the comfort, the wealth, the civilization of the north, in glowing colors — when there rose on the vision of the assembly, gathered in the open air, a horseman of magnificent proportions; and just at the moment of hushed attention, when the voice of Prentiss had ceased and the applause was about to break forth, the horseman exclaimed, " Damn the north! " The sentiment was so much in unison with the habitual feeling of a Mississippi audience that it quenched their enthusiasm, and nothing but respect for the speaker kept them from cheering the horseman.

Prentiss turned upon his lame foot, and said: " Major Moody, will you rein in that horse a moment? " The horseman assented. The orator went on: " Major, the horse on which you ride came from upper Missouri; the saddle that surmounts him came from Trenton, New Jersey; the hat on your head came from Danbury, Connecticut; the boots you wear came from Lynn, Massachusetts; the linen in your shirt is Irish, and Boston made it up; your broadcloth coat is of Lowell manufacture, and was cut in New York; and if today you surrender what you owe the ' damn north ' you would sit stark naked."

A well authenticated Prentiss story told about Natchez, usually with interesting embellishments, is the account of his prosecution of a bedbug. The scene was a backwoods town and a wretched tavern which the lawyers of that circuit were obliged to patronize for the good reason that there was no other place to go. One night when the pests were more murderous than usual Prentiss and his fellow lawyers arose and ordered refreshments sent up to their room. After a few rounds of drinks Prentiss remarked that he had captured one of the murderous scoundrels and prepared to put him on trial for his life. The bug was placed on a rude table in the center of the room and Prentiss acting as prosecuting attorney held his small audience spellbound. The orator arraigned the defendant for high crimes and misdemeanors, with a wealth of classical allusion and excursions into ancient lore, charging the bedbug to be the ancient enemy of man and asking for a verdict of death. The jury voted guilty and the execution of the prisoner followed as day broke and the mockingbirds burst into song.

Prentiss was once asked how he had acquired his fluency and extraordinary diction. His answer is revealing. He said: " When I get to speaking and become excited I'm like a little boy walking through a meadow. When he sees a beautiful butterfly, with its gauzy wings of gold, and starts in pursuit, eager to capture the glittering prize, in the race up springs another and still another until the whole sky is filled with beautiful butterflies, every new one brighter than the others. It's so with me; every fancy starts a new one, till in the pursuit my whole mind is filled with beautiful butterflies."

This orator's weaknesses were such as are common to warm and generous natures in a day when excesses were excused if not condoned. He fought two duels and prepared to fight a third. His conviviality was probably only a little more marked than that of some of his illustrious contemporaries. His fondness for the gaming table was about on a footing with that of his friends and neighbors. His prodigality with money, however, was exceptional. Once, in the old Galt House at Louisville where he was a guest, a great commotion was heard in the hall. Investigation revealed Prentiss having a royally good time rolling half dollars from one end of the hall to the colored waiters at the other and watching them scramble and scrap for the coins. His generous use of his name cost him heavy losses; it was his habit to sign his name on blank notes for the use of his intimate friends and others who had befriended him, often with disastrous results to his fortune. Yet it is doubtful if in this practice he greatly differed from many other southern gentlemen of that free and easy period.

The closing years of Prentiss' life were full of pecuniary disaster and physical suffering, for already disease had invaded his weakened body. Ill fortune pursued him relentlessly. His ample property holdings in Vicksburg became involved in litigation and the Supreme Court ruled against his title claims. This decision ruined him financially. Debts piled up. Death robbed him of a favorite sister. Security notes fell due and there was no money with which to meet them. His physical condition became alarming. Yet he preserved an outward calm, a debonair spirit. The orator was still strong. He spoke at New Orleans and other nearby cities with much of the old-time fire. He tried to withdraw from all speaking activities, but failed; there was no place to stop, no time for rest. If he appeared at a dinner or some public affair where he was not on the program the sight of him set the crowd shouting, " Prentiss! Prentiss! " and nothing would do but he must address the people.

His last speech was for the cause of Cuban independence, to which he was passionately devoted. Scarcely had he finished when he fainted. Stricken in New Orleans he was carried to the St. Charles Hotel where he lay for three days dangerously ill. He asked to be removed to his beloved " Longwood," and by steamer he was taken to Natchez and then tenderly borne to his quiet home and to the midst of his family. There, on July 1, 1850, with his wife holding his hand and the solemn words of the old litany on his lips, " God, the Son . . . Redeemer of the world, have mercy upon us miserable sinners," Seargent S. Prentiss died.

About a mile from Natchez is a plot of ground walled in by gray stones and reached by a flight of steps from the main highway. Great and venerable oaks, hung with moss, stand like sentinels above the gravestones, and a tangle of vines and underbrush gives to the spot a kind of mournful, desolate beauty. The grave of the orator is marked by a simple headstone bearing his name and the dates of his birth and death, followed by the familiar words from the fourteenth chapter of St. John's Gospel, " I am the resurrection and the life; he that believeth on me, though he were dead, yet shall he live."

Comparatively few today know of this sequestered rural burial place, other than the people of Natchez and its vicinity. To millions of his fellow countrymen Seargent S. Prentiss is not even a name, although his generation lifted him up on a high pedestal and all but worshiped him. Yet is his fate so sorry after all? He was showered with sweets in life. He had his red, red roses while his eyes could see their beauty and his being thrill to their perfume. For his frailties, tears and prayers; for his genius and generous heart, a garland of immortelles!

ABRAHAM LINCOLN .

He Lives in Both Words and Deeds

~VII~

ABRAHAM LINCOLN

EXALTED AS IS the place of Abraham Lincoln in the minds of millions, not many think of him as an orator. This may be because what he *did* so greatly transcends what he said. Multitudes think of him as a successful lawyer, an able debater, a wise statesman, the author of the impressive Gettysburg speech and the sublime " second inaugural," but they do not instinctively think of Lincoln as silver-tongued. Yet every student of his life will agree with William E. Barton, one of his best biographers, who says, " Had Abraham Lincoln been everything else that he was and lacked his oratorical powers, he would never have been president of the United States."

Lincoln was the antithesis of Everett whose grace was equaled only by his fluency and charm; he had none of Webster's solemn magnificence; he suffers when compared with the magnetic and imperious Clay; he possessed little of the epigrammatic brilliance and none of the patrician presence of Wendell Phillips, or the gorgeous rhetoric of Ingersoll; nor was there in him a trace of the versatility and grand sweep of Henry Ward Beecher's eloquent periods. Nevertheless for his clarity of statement, powerful logic, quaint illustration, together with his occasional eloquence of a poetic and prophetic quality, this plain, awkward man of the prairies is numbered with those who spoke with the tongues of angels. Professor Robinson * says: " This ' self-educated ' man clothed his mind with the materials of genuine culture. Call it genius or talent, the process of his attainment was that described by Professor Emerton in speaking of the education of Erasmus: ' He was no longer at school, but was simply educating himself by the only pedagogical method which ever yet produced any results anywhere — namely, by the method of his own tireless energy in continuous study and practice.' "

As boy and young man Lincoln was ambitious to excel in public speaking. To further this ambition he made it a point to hear every preacher, lawyer and lecturer who came his way. Not only so, but often he walked or rode horseback many miles to listen to men who had a national reputation as masters of assemblies.

Lincoln's first speech of which we have any record was an announcement at a political gathering of his candidacy for the legislature of Illinois. Picture the scene: A political meeting on the prairies of his adopted state, a crowd of farmers and villagers straggling about a rude platform. The time early in the year 1832. On

* Probably the most valuable book on Lincoln's literary development is Professor Luther Emerson Robinson's *Abraham Lincoln as a Man of Letters* (Chicago, 1918). Dr. Robinson was professor of English in Monmouth College and made an exhaustive word study of the Lincoln speeches, correspondence and state papers. The result is a scholarly account of the growth of a style, vocabulary, diction and poetic quality which are at once the marvel and the despair of critics.

the platform a tall backwoods youth of twenty-three, clad in nondescript garments which ill fitted him, shy, awkward, earnest. He smiles broadly, acknowledges the handclapping, lifts up a long arm and says:

> I presume you all know who I am. I am humble Abraham Lincoln. I have been solicited by many friends to become a candidate for the legislature. My politics are short and sweet like the old woman's dance. I am in favor of a national bank. I am in favor of the internal improvement system, and a high protective tariff. These are my sentiments and political principles. If elected I shall be thankful. If not it will be all the same.

Now this is a good speech, remarkably brief, clear, quaint and informative. Actually it is a summary of a circular that this young politician had made up and distributed among the voters. He was defeated but polled a respectable vote and increased the number of his friends and acquaintances.

Two years later Lincoln was elected to the legislature and served four terms. In this body he spoke frequently, usually to the point, sometimes indulging in sarcasm, and there was a salty tang to his utterance. During his one term in the national House of Representatives, shortly after he arrived in Washington, he wrote to Herndon: " By way of experiment, and of getting the hang of the House, I made a little speech two or three days ago on a post office question of no general interest. I find speaking here and elsewhere almost the same thing. I was about as badly scared and no more than when I speak in court."

Early in his congressional term Lincoln made an extended speech in the House, arraigning President Polk for the Mexican war. He also made a speech on internal improvements, and still another in which he ridiculed the Democratic candidate for president, General Cass. A passage from this latter speech reveals a different Lincoln from the more mature and growing statesman of later years:

> By the way, Mr. Speaker, did you know I am a military man? Yes, sir, in the days of the Black Hawk war, I fought, bled, and came away. Speaking of General Cass' career reminds me of my own. I was not at Stillman's defeat, but I was about as near it as Cass was to Hill's surrender; and like him, I saw the place very soon afterward. It is quite certain I did not break my record, for I had none to break; but I bent a musket pretty badly on one occasion. If Cass broke his record, the idea is that he broke it in desperation; I bent the musket by accident. If General Cass went in advance of me in picking whortle berries, I guess I surpassed him in charges upon wild onions. If he saw any live fighting Indians, it was more than I did; but I had a good many bloody struggles with the mosquitoes; and although I never fainted from the loss of blood, I can truly say I was often very hungry.

There were roars of laughter from the Whigs as Congressman Lincoln indulged in this levity and ridicule.

In some of his speeches of this period and a little earlier, Lincoln indulged in a stilted and artificial eloquence which contrasts strangely with the chaste and grand simplicity of the speeches by which he is known to fame. Here is a specimen of bombast from a campaign speech of Lincoln's in the presidential contest of 1840:

Mr. Lamborn refers to the late elections in the states, and from their results confidently predicts every state in the union will vote for Mr. Van Buren at the next presidential election. Address that argument to cowards and knaves: with the free and the brave it will affect nothing. It may be true; if it must, let it. Many free countries have lost their liberty, and ours may lose hers; but if she shall, be it my proudest plume, not that I was the last to desert, but that I never deserted her. I know that the great volcano at Washington, aroused and directed by the evil spirit that reigns there, is belching forth the lava of political corruption in a current broad and deep, which is sweeping with frightful velocity over the whole length and breadth of the land, bidding fair to leave unscathed no green spot or living thing; while on its bosom are riding, like demons on the wave of hell, the imps of the evil spirit, and fiendishly taunting all those who dare to resist its destroying course with the hopelessness of their efforts; and knowing this, I cannot deny that all may be swept away. Broken by it, I, too, may be; bow to it, I never will. The probability that we may fall in the struggle ought not to deter us from the support of a cause we believe to be just. It shall not deter me. If ever I feel the soul within me elevate and expand to those dimensions not wholly unworthy of its Almighty Architect, it is when I contemplate the cause of my country, deserted by all the world beside, and I standing up boldly alone, hurling defiance at her victorious oppressors. Here, without contemplating consequences, before heaven and in face of the world, I swear eternal fealty to the just cause, as I deem it, of the land of my life, my liberty, and my love. And who that thinks with me will not fearlessly adopt that oath that I take? Let none falter who thinks he is right, and we may succeed. But if after all we should fail, be it so. We still shall have the proud consolation of saying to our consciences, and to the departed shade of our country's freedom, that the cause approved of our judgment, and adored of our hearts, in disaster, in chains, in torture, in death, we never faltered in defending.

Writing of Lincoln's oratorical development Barton says: " In Lincoln's earlier stump speeches he is described as indulging in the familiar oratorical tricks of the time and region. He gesticulated with wide-reaching gestures. He stooped low, and rose to his full height, raising his voice as he ascended, and sometimes accentuating his stature by standing on tiptoe. All this is to be charged up to experience in the career of Lincoln as an orator. He outgrew all these tricks. He stood calmly in his place, and if he moved, he moved with his thoughts, and the movement was natural and not ungraceful. He gesticulated little, and that little, being unstudied, was effective. His whole progress was toward simplicity and effectiveness. His was a very honest type of oratory, and it had weight with his hearers."

Lincoln used some words and phrases in his speeches and correspondence that had a homespun flavor. These, for example: " gone to pot," " sugar-coated," " cat's paw," " scour " as a synonym for " wear," " swap horses while crossing the river." His pronunciation of certain words was eccentric. He pronounced *America,* " Amerikay "; *one* as if it were spelled " own "; *idea* he pronounced in two syllables with accent on the first. When he arose to speak in Cooper Union he addressed cultured Mr. Bryant, the presiding officer, as " Mr. Cheerman." And he pronounced the word *to* as if it were spelled " toe." Most of these oddities of speech were characteristic of the region in which he lived. Dr. Robinson has well said, " A touch of rusticity contributed by birth and environment is to be found in much of his written work, but it enriched his personality and deepened his sympathy and imagination."

During the years between 1848 and 1858 Lincoln grew in mind and in oratorical effectiveness. In these ten years he devoted himself to his law practice and made a name among the legal lights on the old eighth Illinois judicial district. His reputation grew steadily; he read Shakespeare, studied Euclid, devoured eagerly the contents of countless newspapers, worked hard on his cases, and by his quaint and salty stories convulsed many a roomful of companions. He thought he was through with politics, but mighty issues emerged and stirred his soul. In 1858 he accepted the Republican nomination against Stephen A. Douglas for the United States Senate. Two years before Lincoln had returned to the hustings, and his speeches at Bloomington, Galena and other Illinois towns revealed an orator who had simplified his style, making it more direct; who still indulged his sense of humor, but had abandoned sarcasm for something better.

The address of Lincoln on accepting the nomination for the United States Senate was delivered before the Republican state convention at Springfield, June 16, 1858. It is a powerful presentation of the issues of the day, and evidences throughout the development of the candidate in the art of public speaking. Observe the strength and felicity of the opening sentence and the steady movement of the paragraph in exalted argument, working toward a climax:

If we could first know where we are, and whither we are tending, we could better judge what to do, and how to do it.

We are now far into the fifth year since a policy was initiated with the avowed object, and confident promise, of putting an end to slavery agitation. Under the operation of that policy, that agitation not only has not ceased, but has constantly augmented. In my opinion, it will not cease until a crisis shall have been reached and passed. " A house divided against itself cannot stand." I believe this government cannot endure permanently half slave and half free. I do not expect the union to be dissolved; I do not expect the house to fall; but I do expect that it will cease to be divided. It will become all one thing, or all the other. Either the opponents of slavery will arrest the further spread of it, and place it where the public mind shall rest in the belief that it is in the course of ultimate extinction; or its advocates will push it forward till it shall become alike lawful in all the states, old as well as new, north as well as south. Have we no tendency to the latter condition? Let anyone who doubts, carefully contemplate that now almost complete legal combination piece of machinery, so to speak — compounded of the Nebraska doctrine and the Dred Scott decision. Let him consider not only what work the machinery is adapted to do, and how well adapted; but also let him study the history of its construction, and trace, if he can, or rather fail, if he can, to trace the evidences of design and concert of action among its chief architects, from the beginning.

Study the passage that follows, with its courteous yet merciless thrusts at Senator Douglas' position on the paramount issue, slavery. Look at the orator's frequent and effective use of interrogation, a subtle verbal weapon in the hands of a master:

There are those who denounce us openly to their own friends, and yet whisper to us softly that Senator Douglas is the aptest instrument there is with which to effect that object. They wish us to *infer* all, from the fact that he now has a little quarrel with the present head of the dynasty; and that he has regularly voted with us on a single point, upon which he and

we have never differed. They remind us that he is a great
man, and that the largest of us are very small ones. Let this
be granted. " But a living dog is better than a dead lion."
Judge Douglas, if not a dead lion, for this work, is at least a
caged and toothless one. How can he oppose the advances of
slavery? He doesn't care anything about it. His avowed mission is impressing the " public heart " to care nothing about it.
A leading Douglas Democratic newspaper thinks Douglas' superior talent will be needed to resist the revival of the African
slave trade. Does Douglas believe an effort to revive that trade
is approaching? He has not said so. Does he really think so?
But if it is, how can he resist it? For years he has labored to
prove it a sacred right of white men to take Negro slaves into
the new territories. Can he possibly show that it is less a sacred
right to buy them where they can be bought cheapest? And
unquestionably they can be bought cheaper in Africa than
in Virginia.

The Lincoln-Douglas debates made " the Railsplit-
ter " a national figure and a presidential possibility.
As debates, these seven speeches are of inestimable historic value, but they are not orations. The give and
take of the controversial platform is excellent for repartee, clever asides and good stories, but it is not con-
ducive to finished paragraphs or well rounded periods.
Even so, this famed debate shows a Lincoln whose
speaking ability has grown perceptibly, and if his
speeches lack something of Douglas' more Websterian
style, they gain through lucidity and the cross-examina-
tion method in which Lincoln excelled. To this day
the Lincoln-Douglas debates make interesting reading,
and they certainly measurably prepared the lank Illinois lawyer for the heavy speaking responsibilities that
were soon to be his.

Walter B. Stevens, who reported the Lincoln-Douglas debate for his paper, wrote of Lincoln's style of speech in that contest of giants:

His voice was clear, almost shrill. Every syllable was distinct. But his delivery was puzzling to stenographers. He would speak several words with great rapidity, come to the word or phrase he wished to emphasize, and let his voice linger and bear hard on that, and then he would rush to the end of his sentence like lightning. To impress the idea on the mind of his hearers was his aim; not to charm the ear with smooth, flowing words. It was very easy to understand Lincoln. He spoke with great clearness. But his delivery was very irregular. He would devote as much time to the word or two which he wished to emphasize as he did to half a dozen less important words following it.

Lincoln's stories do not often appear in his speeches. For the most part, while there are occasional flashes of humor, anecdotes are scarce. Barton is authority for the statement, gleaned from lawyer associates of Lincoln, that it was only when he failed to have the facts and the evidence on his side that he indulged in stories. Momentous and solemn occasions do not warrant humor save rarely. When a nation faces disunion and war is ravaging a people public speech is bound to be serious, sober and solemn. Lincoln told his stories in private conversation for the most part, and invariably his homely yarns grew out of the situation and were not dragged in. No public speaker who has made a reputation for humor in his speeches has attained the highest office. Crowds delight to listen to jocular speakers, but they are not so keen about voting them into places of vast responsibility.

On the evening of February 27, 1860, Lincoln made
one of the master speeches of his life at Cooper Union,
New York City. It was a testing time for the Illinoisan.
He had before him a cultured and critical audience
such as he had never before addressed. William Cullen
Bryant presided, and on the platform sat some of the
most eminent leaders of New York's commercial and
political life. Lincoln faced that audience handi-
capped by ill-fitting clothes and an awkwardness that
happily disappeared as he got further into his speech.
He closed amid an uproar of applause. Horace Gree-
ley, several years later, pronounced it " the very best
political address to which I have ever listened, and I
have heard some of Webster's grandest." The closing
paragraphs are characteristic of the speech as a whole
— deadly earnest; cogent, logical reasoning:

Nor can we justifiably withhold this on any ground save our
conviction that slavery is wrong. If slavery is right, all words,
acts, laws and constitutions against it are themselves wrong and
should be silenced and swept away. If it is right, we cannot
justly object to its nationality — its universality; if it is wrong,
they cannot justly insist upon its extension — its enlargement.
All they ask we could readily grant, if we thought slavery right;
all we ask they could as readily grant, if they thought it wrong.
Their thinking it right and our thinking it wrong is the precise
fact upon which depends the whole controversy. Thinking it
right, as they do, they are not to blame for desiring its full
recognition as being right; but thinking it wrong, as we do, can
we yield to them? Can we cast our votes with their view, and
against our own? In view of our moral, social and political
responsibilities, can we do this?

Wrong as we think slavery is, we can yet afford to let it alone
where it is, because that much is due to the necessity arising

from its actual presence in the nation; but can we, while our votes will prevent it, allow it to spread into the national territories and to overrun us here in these free states? If our sense of duty forbids this, then let us stand by our duty fearlessly and effectively. Let us be diverted by none of those sophistical contrivances wherewith we are so industriously plied and belabored — contrivances such as groping for some middle ground between the right and the wrong: vain as the search for a man who should be neither a living man nor a dead man; such as a policy of " don't care " on a question about which all true men do care; such as union appeals beseeching true union men to yield to disunionists, reversing the divine rule, and calling not the sinners but the righteous to repentance; such as invocations to Washington, imploring men to unsay what Washington said and undo what Washington did.

Neither let us be slandered from our duty by false accusations against us, nor frightened from it by menaces of destruction to the government, nor of dungeons to ourselves. Let us have faith that right makes might, and in that faith let us to the end dare to do our duty as we understand it.

Monday, February 11, 1861, was a dark, cold day in Illinois, and a drizzly rain was falling. About a thousand persons had gathered at the railway station at Springfield to say good-by to their fellow townsman who was to leave for Washington to be inaugurated president of the United States. Just before the train started, Lincoln appeared on the platform of the rear car, and in a voice choked with emotion he said:

My Friends: No one, not in my situation, can appreciate my feeling of sadness at this parting. To this place, and the kindness of these people, I owe everything. Here I have lived a quarter of a century, and have passed from a young to an old man. Here my children have been born, and one is buried. I now leave, not knowing when or whether ever I may return,

with a task before me greater than that which rested upon
Washington. Without the assistance of that divine Being who
ever attended him, I cannot succeed. With that assistance, I
cannot fail. Trusting in him, who can go with me, and remain
with you, and be everywhere for good, let us confidently hope
that all will yet be well. To his care commending you as I
hope in your prayers you will commend me, I bid you an
affectionate farewell.

This speech is perfect. It has everything to commend
it — artistry and restraint and a deep solemnity, and
a prophetic strain runs through the concluding words.
It foreshadows the Gettysburg address and the " second
inaugural." The orator is coming into his own.

Of the " first inaugural " much could be said in
praise. No president ever faced so momentous and
solemn a responsibility. The union was dissolving.
No man could foresee the end. It was an ordeal, and
right bravely did Lincoln meet it. It is one of his longest speeches, if not the longest. It was addressed particularly to the south, and is, in the main, conciliatory.
It was a constitutional speech, and contains one of the
frankest statements of government of the people that
any American president ever uttered: " This country,
with its institutions, belongs to the people who inhabit
it. Whenever they grow weary of the existing government, they can exercise their constitutional right of
amending it, or their revolutionary right to dismember
or overthrow it."

Yet the speech as a whole was not everywhere favor-
ably received even in the north, though the *New York
Tribune* commented on its simplicity and its kindliness.

In the popular view Lincoln's speech at Gettsyburg, November 19, 1863, is the high-water mark of his oratory, and the view has much to sustain it. That speech was probably the briefest formal utterance to win immortal renown in the history of oratory. But the speech itself cannot be dissociated from the circumstances of its delivery, the emotions of the people at the time, and the personality of the speaker. Lincoln was not the orator of that day. Edward Everett was, and his fame filled the nation. He made the most painstaking preparation, visiting the battlefield weeks before the event, studying every detail of the three days' battle from the official documents. He spoke one hour and fifty-seven minutes without reference to so much as a single note. He was faultlessly attired, noble of presence, graceful in gestures, his voice was of cultured accent, his diction flawless. Everett's speech made a profound impression and stirred his hearers to prolonged applause. The grand oration of the day was over. The President of the United States slowly arose and advanced to the front of the platform. He held a manuscript in his hand, adjusted his spectacles and read, though not slavishly, what he had written for the occasion:

Four score and seven years ago our fathers brought forth on this continent a new nation, conceived in liberty, and dedicated to the proposition that all men are created equal. Now we are engaged in a great civil war, testing whether that nation, or any nation so conceived and so dedicated, can long endure. We are met on a great battlefield of that war. We have come to dedicate a portion of that field, as a final resting place for those who here gave their lives that that nation might live. It is altogether fitting and proper that we should do this. But in a larger sense, we cannot dedicate, we cannot consecrate, we cannot hallow this ground. The brave men, living and dead, who struggled here have consecrated it far above our poor power to add or detract. The world will little note nor long remember what we may say here, but it can never forget what they did here. It is for us the living rather to be dedicated here to the unfinished work which they who fought here have thus far so nobly advanced. It is rather for us to be here dedicated to the great task remaining before us, that from these honored dead we take increased devotion to that cause for which they gave the last full measure of devotion; that we here highly resolve that these dead shall not have died in vain; that this nation, under God, shall have a new birth of freedom, and that government of the people, by the people, and for the people, shall not perish from the earth.

There are contradictory accounts of the reception of the Gettysburg address by the audience. The best opinion based on contemporary comment is that the thousands who heard this brief, beautiful speech were not visibly impressed. This is understandable. For one thing, the contrast between Lincoln and the orator of the day, both in personal appearance and in manner of speaking, was very great. Moreover, the brevity of the speech was astonishing. He was through before he had fairly begun.

Now, it requires a little time for a speaker to create his atmosphere. The audience has to adjust to him, sense his personality, come under his spell. In the case of Lincoln at Gettysburg there was no time for this. What would ordinarily have served as introductory remarks was the speech in its entirety. Moreover, the people were tired, restless. They had been standing for two hours or more.   It is doubtful if any speaker ever faced so difficult a situation as did Abraham Lincoln at Gettysburg.

Lincoln felt that he had failed, and that was probably the opinion of most of those who listened that day to the tall, tired-faced President dressed in somber black.   It was only gradually that the greatness of this speech was recognized, and the first notable praise came from England and the pen of Goldwin Smith in *MacMillan's Magazine* of February, 1865, nearly two years later.   In 1913 another Englishman, Earl Curzon of Kedleston, delivered a lecture before the University of Cambridge on " Modern Parliamentary Eloquence " in which the noble earl said that " the three supreme masterpieces of English eloquence were the toast of William Pitt after the victory at Trafalgar, and Lincoln's two speeches, the Gettysburg address and the Second Inaugural."

It is the opinion of many, which I share, that Abraham Lincoln's supreme speech was the " second inaugural."   It is almost three times the length of the Gettysburg address, and reveals the orator at the peak of his intellectual and spiritual power, chastened by suffering.   It is a specimen of English pure and unde-filed, and entitles Lincoln to a place among the few illustrious orators whose wise and beautiful words live on:

Neither party expected for the war the magnitude or the duration which it has already attained.   Neither anticipated that the cause of the conflict might cease with, or even before the conflict itself should cease.   Each looked for an easier triumph and a result less fundamental and astounding.

Both read the same Bible, and pray to the same God, and each invokes His aid against the other. It may seem strange that any men should dare to ask a just God's assistance in wringing their bread from the sweat of other men's faces. But let us judge not, that we be not judged. The prayer of both could not be answered. That of neither has been answered fully. The Almighty has his own purposes. "Woe unto the world because of offenses, for it must needs be that offenses come, but woe to that man by whom the offense cometh." If we shall suppose that American slavery is one of these offenses, which in the providence of God must needs come, but which, having continued through his appointed time, he now wills to remove, and that he gives to both north and south this terrible war as the woe due to those by whom the offense came, shall we discern there any departure from those divine attributes which the believers in a living God always ascribe to him? Fondly do we hope, fervently do we pray, that this mighty scourge of war may speedily pass away. Yet if God wills that it continue until all the wealth piled by the bondsman's two hundred and fifty years of unrequited toil shall be sunk, and until every drop of blood drawn with the lash shall be paid by another drawn by the sword, as was said three thousand years ago, so still it must be said, The judgments of the Lord are true and righteous altogether.

With malice toward none, with charity for all, with firmness in the right as God gives us to see the right, let us finish the work we are in, to bind up the nation's wounds, to care for him who shall have borne the battle, and for his widow and his orphan, to do all which may achieve and cherish a just and a lasting peace among ourselves and with all nations.

The closing paragraph is Lincoln's finest utterance. It consists of seventy-two fitly spoken words, a single, long, golden sentence, prophetic, sublime; and akin in spirit to One who spake centuries ago in the Palestinian country and died upon a cross.

On several occasions I have listened to my dear old friend former Governor Joseph W. Fifer of Bloomington, Illinois (born in 1840, and still living as this is written) , describe a speech he heard Lincoln make in Bloomington Saturday afternoon, September 4, 1858. I regard it as the most illuminating of all the accounts I have read or heard of Lincoln as a political orator. Here is a part of " Private Joe's " narrative as taken down by a stenographer:

Then Abraham Lincoln got up, and good Lord, I thought he would never get through getting up! He just unfolded and unfolded. Like Saul, son of Kish, " when he stood among the people he was higher than any of the people from his shoulders and upward," as the Bible says. He didn't seem awkward to me, but managed himself elegantly. My brother and I, as boys would, had elbowed our way right up in front of Mr. Lincoln — about ten feet from him — so I caught every syllable and every gesture. His was not a voluminous voice, not a powerful voice. It was what is called a metallic voice, clear, ringing, very penetrating, and I suppose it reached everybody on the outskirts of that immense throng, partly because he enunciated very distinctly.

Everything he was saying seemed to me to gurgle up from some great fountain of sincerity and truth, and he swept that multitude along with him whether they wanted to go or not. I declare to you that for sincerity I never heard such a speech before or since and, boy though I was, I wasn't wrong, for afterward friends of his told me that he didn't " know men as white men or black men or red men, but only as men who were right or men who were wrong."

But at first he didn't seem to me to be handling himself well. He would run out on a sentence, and it wouldn't satisfy him — didn't hit the mark — and he would go back to its beginning and try it again. He did that two or three times, and a man near me said: " Pshaw, that man can't speak! Why didn't they nominate Leonard Swett? " But pretty soon Mr. Lincoln found himself, and that man shut up. I can't give you now a synopsis of that speech, but I remember it was full of short sentences that charged through the audience like a cannon ball going through a cornfield. What's coming now I recall word for word, partly because of the solemn way he said it. " Judge Douglas charges me," he said, " with being in favor of Negro equality. I have never advocated Negro equality. I do not believe the Negro is the equal of the white man. He may not be his equal in color; he is not his equal in education, and he certainly is not his equal in social attainments. But *in the right to eat the bread his own hands have earned he is the equal of Judge Douglas, or of myself, or of any living man."* Now, Abraham Lincoln didn't gesticulate very much, but when he made that great, solemn point he raised his long right arm with the clenched hand on the end of it — high above his head — and he shook it in the air and then brought it vigorously down. And when he did it — it [the governor's voice breaking a little] made the hair on a man's head stand up, and the breath stop in his throat. *He spoke like the prophets of old.*

The graces of an orator's presence, the charm of his voice and manner, are ephemeral and fleeting, however effective they may be at the time; while the grandeur of his thoughts, the magnanimity of his soul and the soundness of his reasoning live after him. It is the substance of his speeches, together with the chaste beauty of a style which matches the sheer nobility of his spirit, that lifts Abraham Lincoln into the small and elect company of the world's supreme masters of public speech.

HENRY W. GRADY

The Young Man Eloquent

VIII

HENRY W. GRADY

OF ALL the southern orators of his day Henry W. Grady was most typical of the school of flowery speech, with Colonel W. C. P. Breckenridge of Lexington, Kentucky, a close second. Not all the great speakers from south of the Mason and Dixon line belonged to the florid school of rhetoric. Certainly John C. Calhoun and Alexander H. Stephens were not of that category; neither was John G. Carlisle, nor " the Lame Lion of Lynchburg," John W. Daniel. Henry Clay, most famed of southern speakers, was marvelously eloquent, but not fanciful or flowery in style. An example of florid oratory in the period following Grady was Governor Robert L. Taylor of Tennessee, of " Love, Laughter and Song " fame. Fully as flowery as Grady, Taylor lacked the Georgian's sense of mission and was less serious in his platform performances.

The eloquent Grady was born in Georgia in 1850; Atlanta was his home for many years, and he died in that city December 23, 1889. Educated at the state University of Georgia and the University of Virginia, he entered the journalistic field, becoming the successful editor and part owner of the most influential paper in the south, the Atlanta *Constitution*. It has been said

that journalism was his profession and oratory an incident, yet his fame and influence came largely through
his eloquence.   The last years of his brief life were
crowded with speeches of every description and he
could accept but a small number of the invitations that
poured in upon him.

What gives significance and permanence to Grady's
oratory is the noble use he made of it as an ambassador
of reconciliation.   He was a boy at the time of the ago-
nizing struggle between the states.   His father, a Confederate soldier, died on the battlefield.   There were
bitterness and rancor in the hearts of many, but not in
the heart of Grady.   He loved the south and he also
loved the nation.   He saw the necessity of creating a
better understanding and a bond of unity between
north and south, and dedicated his life to this worthy
cause.

Grady was of sanguine temperament and looked
upon the brighter side of every subject. His nature was
kindly and he was peculiarly fitted to become the eloquent peacemaker that he was.   His oratory was ornate
with purple patches and flights of fancy.   His style has
been described as " a cannon ball in full flight, fringed
with flowers."   Yet this phrase is not wholly just or descriptive.   In 1887 Grady debated the prohibition issue
with his associate on the *Constitution,* Captain E. P.
Howell, also an eloquent speaker.   A reporter on the
Evening Journal contrasted their oratory in the following description, which is interesting as a record of contemporary impressions:

Howell makes you feel as if he were the commander of an army, waving his sword and saying, " Follow me," and you would follow him to the death; Grady makes you feel like " you want to be an angel and with the angels stand." Howell will march his audience, like an army, through flood and fire and fell; with subtle humor Grady will lead his audience by the still waters where pleasant pastures lie — and there he will " take the wings of the morning and fly to the uttermost parts of the sea." In Howell's march the drumbeat never ceases; in Grady's flights you hear only the cherubim's wings. Howell's eloquence is like a rushing mountain stream that tears every rock and crag from its path, gathering volume as it goes; Grady's is like a cumulus cloud that rises invisible as mist till it unfolds its white banners in the sky. Howell will doubtless deal in statistics; Grady will have figures, but they will not smell of the census. They will take on the pleasing shape that induced one of his reporters to plant a crop of Irish potatoes on a speculation.

There is a distinctly " homey " flavor about Colonel Grady's oratory. He dearly loves to dwell on the good old-fashioned virtues; put triple rainbows around humble toil; halo the simple life; rhapsodize over mother, home and heaven; glorify religion and the life of the spirit. One of the chapters in his *Orations and Speeches* is " A Plea for Prohibition," delivered before eight thousand of his fellow Atlantans November 17, 1887. Not only is it good oratory, but it is a specimen of moral courage, since most of his associates were on the other side of that controversy. No other American orator outside the pulpit, with the possible exception of William Jennings Bryan, put so much religion into his speeches as did the eloquent Georgian. The same quality that gives the poetry of Edgar A. Guest so vast a popular following made the oratory of Colonel Grady loved and appreciated in the southland.

The evangelical fervor and unaffected piety of this paragraph from an oration on " The Solid South," spoken on Thanksgiving day, 1887, at Augusta, Georgia, mirrors the orator's own abiding faith:

The old-time south is fading from observance, and the mellow church bells that called the people to the temples of God are being tabooed and silenced. Let us, my countrymen, here today — yet a homogeneous and God-fearing people — let us highly resolve that we will carry untainted the straight and simple faith — that we will give ourselves to the saving of the old-fashioned, that we will wear in our hearts the prayers we learned at our mother's knee, and seek no better than that which fortified her life through adversity, and led her serene and smiling through the valley of the shadow.

Let us keep sacred the Sabbath of God in its purity, and have no city so great, or village so small, that every Sunday morning shall not stream forth over towns and meadows the golden benediction of the bells, as they summon the people to the churches of their fathers, and ring out in praise of God and the power of his might. Though other people are led into the bitterness of unbelief, or into the stagnation of apathy and neglect — let us keep these two states in the current of the sweet old-fashioned, that the sweet rushing waters may lap their sides, and everywhere from their soil grow the tree, the leaf whereof shall not fade and the fruit whereof shall not die, but the fruit whereof shall be meat, and the leaf whereof shall be healing.

Colonel Grady's platform style influenced noticeably the public speaking of the south in his generation, and is still discernible in the oratory of that section. The flowers and fancies of his rhetoric have been widely imitated, and alas, not always with the Grady intellectual and reasoning content. In my college days in Lexington, Kentucky, I once heard a preacher use a striking illustration, so unusual and of such length that I fell to speculating where the speaker had picked it up, satisfied it was not original with him. Years afterward I found the incident in Colonel Grady's speech on "The South and Her Problems," given at the state fair at Dallas, October 26, 1887, and probably repeated by the orator on other occasions. The passage is too long to reproduce here in its entirety. It opens with a vivid description of a soldier severely wounded on the field of battle; a surgeon bent over him and said, "I believe if this poor fellow lives to sundown tomorrow he will get well." The sufferer repeated this phrase over and over to himself, and beginning with a vision of his home, recalled the various members of his family. We take up the story at the point where memories of his father come to him:

And he thought of the old father, patient in prayer, bending lower and lower every day under his load of sorrow and old age.

"If I but live till sundown, I shall see him again and wind my strong arm about his feeble body, and his hands shall rest upon my head while the unspeakable healing of his blessing falls into my heart."

And he thought of the little children that clambered on his knees and tangled their little hands into his heartstrings, making to him such music as the world shall not equal or heaven surpass.

"If I live till sundown, they shall again find my parched lips with their warm mouths, and their little fingers shall run once more over my face."

And he thought of his old mother, who gathered these children about her and breathed her old heart afresh in their brightness and attuned her old lips anew to their prattle, that she might live till her big boy came home.

" If I live till sundown, I will see her again, and I will rest my head at my old place on her knees, and weep away all memory of this desolate night." And the Son of God, who died for men, bending from the stars, put the hand that had been nailed to the cross on the ebbing life and held on the stanch until the sun went down and the stars came out and shone down in the brave man's heart and blurred in his glistening eyes, and the lanterns of the surgeons came and he was taken from death to life.

It takes skill to use a story of such length and nature, and skill also to find application as Colonel Grady did, in likening to the wounded soldier the prostrate south struggling to rise out of her defeat, and over all, as ally, the eternal God, stanching her wounds and bidding her to stand upon her feet.   Not many could do this effectively and maintain mastery of their hearers the while, but Grady did.

The speech that put the name of Colonel Grady on a million tongues and won him national fame was delivered in New York City in 1886, just twenty years after the ending of the war.   The occasion was the banquet of the New England Society.   It was an unusual opportunity, astir with possibilities, and the sensitive speaker was fully aware of all that was at stake.   Referring afterward to the event, Grady said: " When I found myself on my feet, every nerve in my body was strung as tight as a fiddle string and all tingling.   I knew then that I had a message for that assemblage.   As soon as I opened my mouth it came rushing out."   The effect

of the speech was sensational and Grady's oratorical
fame, hitherto largely sectional, became nation-wide
over night.   I quote liberally from this celebrated
speech:

My friend, Dr. Talmage, has told you that the typical
American has yet to come.   Let me tell you that he has already
come.   Great types, like valuable plants, are slow to flower and
fruit.   But from the union of these colonists, Puritans and
Cavaliers, from the straightening of their purposes and the
crossing of their blood, slow perfecting through a century, came
he who stands as the first typical American, the first who comprehended within himself all the strength and gentleness, all
the majesty and grace, of this republic — Abraham Lincoln.
He was the sum of Puritan and Cavalier, for in his ardent nature were fused the virtues of both, and in the depths of his
great soul the faults of both were lost.   He was greater than the
Puritan, greater than the Cavalier, in that he was American,
and that in his honest form were first gathered the vast and
thrilling forces of his ideal government, charging it with such
tremendous meaning and elevating it above human suffering,
that martyrdom, though infamously aimed, came as a fitting
crown to a life consecrated from the cradle to human liberty.
Let us, each cherishing the traditions and honoring his fathers,
build with reverent hands to the type of this simple but sublime life, in which all types are honored, and in our common
glory as Americans there will be plenty and to spare for your
forefathers and for mine.

Dr. Talmage has drawn for you, with a master's hand, the
picture of your returning armies.   He has told you how, in the
pomp and circumstance of war, they came back to you, marching with proud and victorious tread, reading their glory in a
nation's eyes!   Will you bear with me while I tell you of another army that sought its home at the close of the late war? —
An army that marched home in defeat and not in victory, in
pathos and not in splendor, but in glory that equaled yours,

and to hearts as loving as ever welcomed heroes home! Let me picture to you the footsore Confederate soldier, as, buttoning up his faded gray jacket, the parole which was to bear testimony to his children of his fidelity and faith, he turned his face southward from Appomattox in April, 1865. Think of him as, ragged, half starved, heavyhearted, enfeebled by want and wounds, having fought to exhaustion, he surrenders his gun, wrings the hands of his comrades in silence, and lifting his tearstained and pallid face for the last time to the graves that dot old Virginia hills, pulls his gray cap over his brow and begins the slow and painful journey. . . .

What does he do — this hero in gray with a heart of gold? Does he sit down in sullenness and despair? Not for a day. Surely God, who had stripped him of his prosperity, inspired him in his adversity. As ruin was never before so overwhelming, never was restoration swifter. The soldier stepped from the trenches into the furrow; horses that had charged federal guns marched before the plow, and fields that ran red with human blood in April were green with the harvest in June; women reared in luxury cut up their dresses and made breeches for their husbands, and with a patience and heroism that fit women always as a garment gave their hands to work. . . .

This message, Mr. President, comes to you from consecrated ground. Every foot of soil about the city in which I live is sacred as a battleground of the republic. Every hill that invests it is hallowed to you by the blood of your brothers who died for your victory, and doubly hallowed to us by the blood of those who died hopeless, but undaunted, in defeat — sacred soil to all of us, rich with memories that make us purer and stronger and better, silent but stanch witnesses in its red desolation of the matchless valor of American hearts and the deathless glory of American arms, speaking an eloquent witness in its white peace and prosperity to the indissoluble union of American states and the imperishable brotherhood of the American people.

Grady spiced his speeches with humor, and even in his epoch-making oration before the New England Society of New York he had the temerity to tell this story — a story that still bobs up from time to time: " There was an old preacher once who told some boys of the Bible lesson he was going to read in the morning. The boys, finding the place, glued together the connecting pages. The next morning he read on the bottom of one page, ' When Noah was one hundred and twenty years old he took unto himself a wife who was ' — then turning the page — ' 140 cubits long, 40 cubits wide, built of gopher wood, and covered with pitch inside and out.' The old preacher was naturally puzzled at this. He read it again, verified it, and then said, ' My friends, this is the first time I ever met this in the Bible, but I accept this as an evidence of the assertion that we are fearfully and wonderfully made.' "

Again, in the introduction to his impromptu speech at Plymouth Rock, in 1889, his last public utterance, Colonel Grady said: " I am a talker by inheritance, my father was an Irishman, my mother was a woman. Both talked, I come by it honestly."

The optimism of Colonel Grady is everywhere discernible in his speeches. His faith in the American republic was unshaken and unshakable. Listen to these sentences taken from his oration " Against Centralization," delivered before the literary societies of the University of Virginia, June 25, 1889:

Let it be understood in my parting words to you that I am no pessimist as to this republic. I always bet on sunshine in

America. I know that my country has reached the point of perilous greatness, and that strange forces not to be measured or comprehended are hurrying her to heights that dazzle and blind all mortal eyes — but I know that beyond the uttermost glory is enthroned the Lord God Almighty, and that when the hour of her trial has come, he will lift up his everlasting gates and bend down above her in mercy and in love. For with her he has surely lodged the ark of his covenant with the sons of men. Emerson wisely said, " Our whole history looks like the last effort of divine Providence in behalf of the human race." And the republic will endure. Centralism will be checked, and liberty saved — plutocracy overthrown and equality restored. . . . And bending down humbly as Elisha did, and praying that my eyes shall be made to see, I catch the vision of this republic, its mighty forces in balance, and its unspeakable glory falling on all its children, chief among the federation of English-speaking people, plenty streaming from its borders, and light from its mountaintops, working out its mission under God's approving eye, until the dark continents are opened and the highways of earth established and the shadows lifted, and the jargon of the nations stilled and the perplexities of Babel straightened — and under one language, one liberty, and one God, all the nations of the world hearkening to the American drumbeat and girding up their loins, shall march amid the breaking of the millennial dawn into the paths of righteousness and of peace!

It would be ungenerous to question whether Colonel Grady would make such a speech today, or any time since 1920 and the era of the great disillusionment. The likelihood is that he could and would still play upon this strain, which previous to the World War ran riotously through the speeches of American preachers, lecturers and politicians. Yet it is true that in his day Colonel Grady was fully alive to subversive tendencies

and perils that threatened his country.   He saw the
dangers from afar and called on his beloved in the south
to supply the antidote — religion!

Grady died in his glorious prime, thirty-nine years
old — died in the great old Faith in which he had lived
and which he had so adorned.

HENRY WARD BEECHER

The Shakespeare of the Pulpit

IX

HENRY WARD BEECHER

A VAST HALL, filled with shouting, hissing, hooting men, some brandishing their arms and shaking their fists at an eloquent speaker who is attempting to make himself heard above the tumult. The speaker is short and rotund of body, with a great head and long locks falling over his coat collar. His mobile face is now stern, now smiling, and his resonant voice, husky from much use, roars and thunders:

Now, let us consider the prospect. If the south becomes a slave empire, what relation will it have to you as a customer? [A voice: " Or any other man." Laughter.] It would be an empire of twelve million of people. Now, of these, eight million are white, and four million are black. [A voice: " How many have you got? " Applause and laughter. Another voice: " Free your own slaves."] Consider that one third of the whole are the miserably poor, unbuying blacks. [Cries of " No, no! " " Yes, yes! " and interruptions.] You do not manufacture much for them. [Hisses, " Oh! " " No."] You have not got machinery coarse enough. [Laughter, and " No."] Your labor is too skilled by far to manufacture bagging and linsey-woolsey. [A southerner: " We are going to free them, every one."] Then you and I agree exactly. [Laughter.] One other third consists of a poor, unskilled, degraded white population; and the remaining one third, which is a large allowance, we will say, intelligent and rich.

Now here are twelve million of people, and only one third of them are customers that can afford to buy the kind of goods that you bring to market. [Interruption and uproar.] My friends, I saw a man once, who was a little late at a railway station, chase an express train. He did not catch it. [Laughter.] If you are going to stop this meeting, you have got to stop it before I speak; for after I have got the things out, you may chase as long as you please — you would not catch them. [Laughter and interruption.] But there is luck in leisure; I'm going to take it easy. [Laughter.] Two thirds of the population of the southern states today are non-purchasers of English goods. [A voice: " No, they are not "; " No, no! " and uproar.] Now you must recollect another fact — namely, that this is going on clear through to the Pacific ocean; and if by sympathy or help you establish a slave empire, you sagacious Britons — [" Oh, oh! " and hooting] — if you like it better, then, I will leave the adjective out — [laughter, " Hear! " and applause] — are busy in favoring the establishment of an empire from ocean to ocean that should have fewest customers and the largest non-buying population. [Applause, " No, no! " A voice: " I thought it was the happy people that populated fastest."] . . .

And now in the future it is the work of every good man and patriot not to create divisions, but to do the things that will make for peace. [" Oh, oh! " and laughter.] On our part it shall be done. [Applause and hisses, and " No, no! "] On your part it ought to be done; and when in any of the convulsions that come upon the world, Great Britain finds herself struggling singlehanded against the gigantic powers that spread oppression and darkness — [applause, hisses, and uproar] — there ought to be such cordiality that she can turn and say to her firstborn and most illustrious child, " Come! " [" Hear, hear! " applause, tremendous cheers and uproar.] I will not say that England cannot again, as hitherto, singlehanded manage any power — [applause and uproar] — but I will say that England and America together for religion and liberty — [a voice: " Soap, soap," uproar, and great applause] — are a match for the world. [Applause; a voice: " They don't want any more soft soap."] Now, gentlemen and ladies — [a voice: " Sam Slick "; and another voice: " Ladies and gentlemen, if you please "] — when I came I was asked whether I would answer questions, and I very readily consented to do so, as I had in other places; but I will tell you it was because I expected to have the opportunity of speaking with some sort of ease and quiet. [A voice: " So you have."] I have for an hour and a half spoken against a storm — [" Hear, hear! "] — and you yourselves are witnesses that, by the interruption, I have been obliged to strive with my voice, so that I no longer have the power to control this assembly. [Applause.] And although I am in spirit perfectly willing to answer any question, and more than glad of the chance, yet I am by this very unnecessary opposition tonight incapacitated physically from doing it. Ladies and gentlemen, I bid you good evening.

The place is Liverpool, the date October 16, 1863, and the speaker Henry Ward Beecher, in one of his most dramatic oratorical triumphs.*

Theodore Parker once said that Lyman Beecher was the father of more brains than any man in America. And Lyman's son, Henry Ward, remarked that at his best his father was greater than all of his family put together. Take a good look at the head of the house of Beecher. Born in 1775, son of David Beecher, blacksmith and farmer, he was a frail child, but by much outdoor activity, hard work on the farm, and hunting and

* Justice Roger A. Prior of the Supreme Court of New York state, who had been in his youth on the staff of General Robert E. Lee, said it was the opinion of General Lee that, had it not been for *Uncle Tom's Cabin* and Henry Ward Beecher's speeches in the British Isles, the Confederacy could have received the recognition of Great Britain and France, with all that would have meant for the south in moral and material aid.

fishing for diversion, he became something of an athlete. He graduated from Yale College and began his ministerial career with great ardor. In person he was tall, with handsome features. He was unconventional, independent, and a born reformer. He fought dueling, intemperance and gambling at a time when most of the prominent pulpits were silent on such subjects. He handled infidelity, atheism and irreligion without gloves, yet he had a heart of gold for the human beings whom he sought to save to the good life.

Back home after his Sunday evening sermons Dr. Beecher would amuse himself by fiddling until he was tired, and then, to the delight of his children, would remove his shoes and dance a hornpipe. Mrs. Beecher objected to his dancing, but only because his gyrations wore out his socks, for money was always scarce in Lyman Beecher's home. Yet this buoyant, volatile prophet of the Most High wrote learned books, advanced ideas that brought charges of heresy, fought slavery with every ounce of his energy, became president of Lane Seminary at Cincinnati, and fathered a vivacious brood that made history.

Checking up on the Beecher family one discovers that they produced one hundred and thirty-seven books and innumerable pamphlets. They lived in fifteen different states and forty-five towns or cities, and their average age, omitting George who died young, was eighty-two and a fraction. This remarkable record is not duplicated by any other American family; the unrecorded ministries of the Beechers would probably fill an encyclopedia.

Out of Lyman Beecher's parsonage came the most famous preacher of his day, and one of the most celebrated of all times, "the Shakespeare of the pulpit," Henry Ward Beecher. He was a rosy-cheeked, pudgy little boy in the days when his father resided at Litchfield. It was there he wrote his first letter:

" Der Sister
We ar at wel. Ma haz a baby. The old sow has six pigs."

He was thirteen when his father moved to Boston. There he loved to watch the ships in the harbor and listen to the music of the church bells on Sunday morning. He experienced conversion, entered Amherst College, threw himself with zest into the student religious activities, showed remarkable ability in public speech, graduated in 1834, attended Lane Seminary whence he graduated in 1837, the year his father, its president, was tried for heresy. Finally he entered the ministry. His first pastorate was at Lawrenceburg, Indiana, where his church had twenty members — nineteen women and one man. He was his own janitor, treasurer, Sunday school superintendent and choir leader, but he made his humble church a center of life, so that it was filled to overflowing. He became minister of the Second Presbyterian Church of Indianapolis, where his reputation grew prodigiously. In 1847 he went to the ministry of a new congregation in Brooklyn, and for forty-one turbulent, dramatic years he made the pulpit of Plymouth Church a throne of spiritual and political power.

Henry Ward Beecher was the incomparable orator of

the pulpit. The range of his eloquence was astonishing. He touched every chord of human emotions. He was marvelously gifted in public prayer and, like all the Beechers, a bold and independent thinker.

In appearance at this time he was short and stocky of build, with a leonine head, his long hair falling in ringlets over his shoulders, an orator's mouth, and a voice of organ tones and range. His vitality was immense; his personality vibrant and magnetic. Let us listen to the Shakespeare of the pulpit on an occasion notable in the annals of our country.

The scene of this triumph was Fort Sumter at the raising of the Stars and Stripes over the old fortress April 14, 1865. A party of his friends — Theodore Tilton, Dr. R. S. Storrs, William Lloyd Garrison and other distinguished citizens — accompanied the orator as guests of the government. The ceremony was impressive, with the setting of drama which Beecher so dearly loved. " He stood on a heap of stones," writes Paxton Hibben, " his slightly graying hair flying in the wind, his full face flushed by the southern sun, his sonorous words echoing back from the battered walls." He had made careful preparation and the result was one of his most effective orations.

Ladies and Gentlemen: On this solemn and joyful day, we again lift to the breeze our fathers' flag, now again the banner of *the United States,* with the fervent prayer that God would crown it with honor, protect it from treason, and send it down to our children, with all the blessings of civilization, liberty, and religion. Terrible in battle, may it be beneficent in peace. Happily, no bird or beast of prey has been inscribed upon it. The stars that redeem the night from darkness, and the beams of red light that beautify the morning, have been united upon its folds. As long as the sun endures, or the stars, may it wave over a nation neither enslaved nor enslaving. Once, and but once, has treason dishonored it. In that insane hour, when the guiltiest and bloodiest rebellion of time hurled its fires upon this fort, you, sir [turning to General Anderson], and a small heroic band, stood within these now crumbled walls, and did gallant and just battle for the honor and defense of the nation's banner.

. . . .

We exult, not for a passion gratified, but for a sentiment victorious; not for temper, but for conscience; not as we devoutly believe that *our* will is done, but that God's will hath been done. We should be unworthy of that liberty entrusted to our care, if, on such a day as this, we sullied our hearts by feelings of aimless vengeance; and equally unworthy, if we did not devoutly thank Him who hath said, *Vengeance is mine, I will repay, saith the Lord,* that he hath set a mark upon arrogant rebellion, ineffaceable while time lasts!

Since this flag went down on that dark day, who shall tell the mighty woes that have made this land a spectacle to angels and men? The soil has drunk blood, and is glutted. Millions mourn for millions slain; or, envying the dead, pray for oblivion. Towns and villages have been razed. Fruitful fields have turned back to wilderness. It came to pass, as the prophet said: *The sun was turned to darkness, and the moon to blood.* The course of law was ended. The sword sat chief magistrate in half the nation; industry was paralyzed; morals corrupted; the public weal invaded by rapine and anarchy; whole states ravaged by avenging armies. The world was amazed. The earth reeled. When the flag sank here, it was as if political night had come, and all beasts of prey had come forth to devour.

That long night has ended! And for this returning day we have come from afar, to rejoice and give thanks. No more war! No more accursed secession! No more slavery, that spawned them both!

And so on for a full hour, closing with a benediction: " In the name of God, we lift up our banner, and dedicate it to peace, union and liberty, now and forevermore. Amen."

Before Beecher and his companions left South Carolina following the flag-raising ceremonies the awful news of the President's assassination reached them, and their elation was turned to sorrow. The following Sunday Plymouth Church was filled to capacity and hundreds were turned away. Beecher spoke on the " Effect of the Death of Lincoln." The time for preparation was short, but his creative mind functioned with its usual fecundity, was indeed stimulated by the tragedy, for he was never more impressive, pictorial, dramatic, eloquent. I nowhere recall so vivid a description of a stunned and sorrow-swept people. Observe the use of figurative language, carefully chosen, and picture the general effect on a nation paralyzed with grief:

The blow brought not a sharp pang. It was so terrible that at first it stunned sensibility. Citizens were like men awakened at midnight by an earthquake and bewildered to find everything that they were accustomed to trust wavering and falling. The very earth was no longer solid. The first feeling was the least. Men waited to get straight to feel. They wandered in the streets as if groping after some impending dread, or undeveloped sorrow, or someone to tell them what ailed them. They met each other as if each would ask the other, " Am I awake, or do I dream? " There was a piteous helplessness. Strong men bowed down and wept. Other and common griefs belonged to someone in chief; this belonged to all. It was each and every man's. Every virtuous household in the land felt as if its firstborn were gone. Men were bereaved and walked for days as if a corpse lay unburied in their dwellings. There was nothing else to think of. They could speak of nothing but that; and yet of that they could speak only falteringly. All business was laid aside. Pleasure forgot to smile. The city for nearly a week ceased to roar. The great leviathan lay down, and was still. Even avarice stood still, and greed was strangely moved to generous sympathy and universal sorrow. Rear to his name monuments, found charitable institutions, and write his name above their lintels; but no monument will ever equal the universal, spontaneous, and sublime sorrow that in a moment swept down lines and parties, and covered up animosities, and in an hour brought a divided people into unity of grief and indivisible fellowship of anguish. . . .

This is an excellent example of Beecher's command of language and of the play of his riotous imagination. Especially good is, " The great leviathan lay down, and was still." Nobody but Beecher would have thought of that figure, or if so, no other orator would dare to use it.

And now the grand peroration, moving to a sonorous climax, sustained to the very last word:

Dead, dead, dead, he yet speaketh. Is Washington dead? Is Hampden dead? Is David dead? Is any man that ever was fit to live dead? Disenthralled of flesh, and risen in the unobstructed sphere where passion never comes, he begins his illimitable work. His life now is grafted upon the infinite, and will be fruitful as no earthly life can be. Pass on, thou that hast overcome. Your sorrows, O people, are his peace. Your bells and bands and muffled drums sound triumph in his ear. Wail and weep here; God made it echo joy and triumph there. Pass on.

Four years ago, O Illinois, we took from your midst an untried man and from among the people. We return him to

you a mighty conqueror. Not thine any more, but the nation's; not ours, but the world's. Give him place, O ye prairies.
In the midst of this great continent his dust shall rest, a sacred treasure to myriads who shall pilgrim to that shrine to
kindle anew their zeal and patriotism. Ye winds that move
over the mighty places of the west, chant his requiem. Ye
people, behold a martyr whose blood, as so many articulate
words, pleads for fidelity, for law, for liberty.

Chauncey Depew, the famous orator and after-dinner
speaker, knew Beecher intimately and heard him often.
He has left the testimony that the Brooklyn preacher
" teemed with ideas all the time," and that he " found
more material in twenty-four hours than he could use.
. . . While other orators were preparing, he seemed to
be seeking occasions for talking and drawing from an
overflowing reservoir. Frequently he would spend an
hour with a crowd of admirers, just talking to them on
any subject which might be uppermost in his mind. I
knew an authoress who was always present at these
gatherings, who took copious notes and reproduced
them with great fidelity. There were circles of Beecher
worshipers in many towns and in many states. This
authoress used to come to New Haven in my senior year
at Yale, and in a circle of Beecher admirers, which I was
permitted to attend, would reproduce these informal
talks of Mr. Beecher. He was the most ready orator,
and with his almost feminine sympathies and emotional
nature would add immensely to his formal speech by
ideas which would occur to him in the heat of delivery,
or with comment upon conversations which he had
heard on the way to church or meeting."

Speaking often to turbulent crowds Beecher was exceedingly clever at repartee. Once when he was in the midst of an impassioned passage, a drunken man in the balcony waved his arms and crowed like a rooster. Instantly Beecher stopped, took out his watch, and remarked: " What, morning already? I wouldn't have believed it, but the instincts of the lower animal are infallible." The crowd roared; the orator caught up the threads of his discourse and went on as if nothing had happened. Again, and this time in England, when he was addressing an audience sympathetic to the south, a heckler shouted, " I thought you said you of the north would whip the south in six months; why haven't you done it? " Instantly Beecher shouted back above the tumult, " Because we are fighting Americans, not Britishers." And again the audience expressed its appreciation. On another occasion in this country, after he had said in a speech to a vast audience, " The voice of the people is the voice of God," from the gallery a man shrilled, " The voice of the people is the voice of a fool." Beecher: " I said the voice of the people, not the voice of one man." And so on and on — Beecher was never caught off guard. And how he loved the crowds, the excitement, the sheer thrill of a hostile audience!

Henry Ward never had any trouble keeping his congregation awake. Plymouth Church in his day was a poor place to go for a nap. He dearly loved to shock his hearers out of their Sabbath somnolency by exploding verbal bombs about their heads. What a charge he let loose that day when at the close of a sermon on " The Love of God " he volleyed:

When I come up before the eternal Judge, and say all aglow, " My Lord and my God," will he turn to me and say: " You did not come up the right road . . . go down "? I, to the face of Jehovah, will stand and say: " God! I won't go to hell; I will go to heaven; I love Thee. Now damn me if Thou canst. I love Thee." And God shall say, and the heavens flame with double and triple rainbows, and echo with joy: " Dost thou love? Enter in and be blessed forever." Let us pray.

It took courage to talk that way from a pulpit in Beecher's day.

How did this gifted orator prepare his speeches and sermons? What method did he follow? Certainly he respected none of the prescribed rules. He was unconventional in everything, and while he was always refreshing his mind through reading and observation, he kept no regular study or office hours. Here is Beecher's own account of his methods in so far as he had any:

I always have floating in my head half-formed thoughts I would like to utter. Saturday is my day of rest. I am apt to spend it on my farm at Peekskill under the trees. I sleep soundly Saturday night; I sleep vicariously for my congregation. After breakfast I go into my study, feel of my different themes, the one that is ripe I pluck, select my text, organize my thought, and go into the pulpit with my theme fresh, my mind and heart full of it.

Nobody but a genius could follow such a course, and woe to the young theologian who attempts it. This preacher recognized no rules but his own and frequently broke these with a disregard that was daring and dangerous. He was unlike any who went before him, and he had no successor.

Beecher's preaching was not only distinguished by

versatility but also by freshness and originality of thought. Preaching on " What is Religion? " Sunday morning, August 23, 1874, at the Twin Mountain House in the White mountains, New Hampshire, he took as text II Tim. 2:19: " Nevertheless the foundation of God standeth sure, having this seal, the Lord knoweth them that are his." In the course of this sermon Beecher said:

So God created the church; but whether it should be Presbyterian, or Methodist, or Baptist, or Congregationalist, or Episcopalian, or Roman Catholic — God has never troubled himself about that, though his zealous disciples have. The form of the instrument of religion is not a part of his decrees. He no more ordained that divine worship should be carried on in certain fixed ways than he ordained that men who live by agriculture should harrow or furrow their fields. Agriculture does not stand on the machines which it employs, but on the necessity of men to eat. When God made men hungry he foreordained agriculture. And in the matter of the church, it does not stand on its ordinances.

But do not think that I am speaking contemptuously of these things. What I desire to be understood as saying is that men have no business to worship an ordinance. I say that men have no right to make an idol of the church, or of Sunday, or of the Bible, or of anything that is in itself an instrument. Religion is something other than the instrument by which it is produced.

Do I say my prayers to the schoolhouse? No. And yet, I believe in intelligence; and the school is simply an instrument by which we develop that intelligence. Do I say my prayers to the arithmetic, the geography, and the grammar? No. I think they are useful; but I would kick them every one out of the house if you were to tell me that I must say my prayers to them. They are my servants, my helps, but not my masters.

And so, when men open the doors of the sanctuary on Sunday, the church is not my master: I am its master, for I am a son of God. It is simply the chariot which he has sent to carry me on my journey.

Beecher the orator sometimes offended against good taste. His sister Catherine said she never heard him preach without his sinning in this respect. In a political speech in support of Grover Cleveland against James G. Blaine, Beecher was reported in the *New York Sun,* October 29, 1884, as saying: " If every man in New York state tonight who has broken the Seventh Commandment voted for Cleveland, he would be elected by two hundred thousand majority. There are men in Brooklyn who will say, ' I have been bumming with Cleveland at night.' I will say to any such man, ' You were bumming on your own hook and were so drunk you couldn't see who you were bumming with.' " *

Rather unusual language for a preacher, but then this preacher was himself unusual.

Henry Ward Beecher was approaching sixty when he became engulfed in a tidal wave of sensational publicity — a scandal growing out of a charge of adultery with Elizabeth, the wife of Theodore Tilton, his one-time friend and co-worker. If one wishes to see the seamiest account of this case he should read *An American Portrait,* by Paxton Hibben; and if he would peruse the most charitable interpretation of the sordid episode he should read chapters twenty and twenty-one in Lyman

* Quoted by Paxton Hibben in *Henry Ward Beecher, An American Portrait* (1927), p. 346.

Beecher Stowe's *Saints, Sinners and Beechers,* which
appeared in 1934. The charges of Mr. Tilton resulted
in a lawsuit lasting many months. The jury finally dis-
agreed, standing nine to four for acquittal.

Edward Eggleston is quoted by Lyman Abbott as saying concerning Henry Ward Beecher, " I never knew
a person who knew man so well, and men so ill."
Beecher's sister Harriet wrote: " My brother is hope-
lessly generous and confiding. His inability to believe
evil is something incredible and so has come all this
suffering." Theodore Bacon, in his *Life of Leonard
Bacon,* quotes this remark made by Beecher himself to
his lawyers when they were apologizing for disturbing
him on Sunday about some matter relating to the case:
" Gentlemen, we have good authority for holding that
it is lawful to draw up an ass from a pit on the Sabbath
day. There never was a bigger ass or a deeper pit."
One gratefully takes leave of a painful chapter in this
great preacher's life and drops the veil of charity over a
scandal that shook the nation.

In his old age Lyman Beecher came to live with his
son at Brooklyn, and Sunday after Sunday sat on the
front seat and listened with delight to the gifted
preacher. Occasionally, Henry would invite his father
into the pulpit and the old man would speak briefly to
the congregation. One day toward the last of his life
he was in the pulpit and stood up to say a few words.
He began with much of his old-time eloquence and
clarity of thought, but soon his mind began to wander
pitifully. Henry Ward came to the rescue, put his
hand on Lyman's shoulder, led him gently back to a

chair, and turning to the people he said, as only Henry Ward Beecher could say:

My father is like a man who has lived in one house all of his life and is just about to leave it for a better dwelling, and who goes around from room to room, remembering what occurred there in days gone by. Every room is sacred. Here the children played and slept. This was mother's room. Here was where a little girl sickened and died. And now my father is about ready to leave this old house for his new home, a house not made with hands eternal in the heavens!

Henry Ward Beecher continued his ministry, still lecturing, still writing, preaching twice a Sunday in Plymouth Church, up to Sunday evening, February 27, 1887. No one imagined that it was his last sermon; but it was. Following the service and an act of kindness to two little street gamins who, attracted by the bright lights and the music, had wandered into the church, Beecher went home to die. Brooklyn and a great section of the nation mourned his passing. A thousand editorials were written with Beecher as theme. His body lay in state in the church where for forty years he had poured out a floodtide of golden speech, the bare walls banked with flowers. Fifty thousand people, of every walk of life, and representing many creeds and races, passed in line to look upon his face.

Lyman Beecher's most famous son had finished his course.

ROBERT G. INGERSOLL

A Painter in Words

ROBERT G. INGERSOLL

O F ALL the eloquent speakers America has produced, the most gorgeous rhetorician was Robert
G. Ingersoll. He possessed all the qualities that are
required for the perfect orator: a commanding presence; a melodious voice of great flexibility; a mind
stored with the treasures of literature and stimulated
by wide travel; and an imagination as magnificent and
riotous in coloring as one of Lake Michigan's " million
dollar sunsets." Of this orator Henry Ward Beecher
said, " He is the most brilliant speaker of the English
tongue of all men on this globe." Another contemporary, referring to Ingersoll's eulogy on Roscoe Conk-
ling, wrote, " He was as effective as Demosthenes, as
polished as Cicero, as ornate as Burke, as scholarly as
Gladstone."

It was in a Presbyterian manse in Dresden, New
York, August 11, 1833, that the man who all his life
seemed to be against the churches was born. John
Ingersoll, his father, was a well educated clergyman,
and in his early days orthodox. Nor is it true that in
later years the father and this son were estranged,
though John Ingersoll must have been many times
deeply concerned over the course his eloquent son

chose and followed to the end. Of his father Robert G.
wrote: " He was grand enough to say to me that I had
the same right to my opinion that he had to his. He
was great enough to tell me to read the Bible for myself,
to be honest with myself, and if after reading it, I concluded it was not the word of God, that it was my duty
to say so."

Nor is it true that the preacher-father's harshness
made a rebel out of his son. Colonel Ingersoll gave that
story the lie. He wrote: " My father was a kind and
loving man. He loved his children tenderly and in-
tensively. There was no sacrifice he would not and did
not make for them. . . . My father was infinitely better than the religion he preached. And these stories
about his unkindness are maliciously untrue."

The Ingersolls moved to Illinois in 1845, and in 1853
took residence in Marion, where Robert commenced
the study of law in the office of Willis Allen. Two years
later he settled in Shawneetown and there opened a law
office with his brother Ebon Clark Ingersoll. Five years
later the brothers moved to Peoria, where they continued to practice and where Robert resided until his
removal to Washington in 1877 and to New York in
1885, where he died July 21, 1899. He served as colonel
of cavalry in the Civil War, and in 1866 was attorney
general of Illinois. A delegate to the National Republican Convention of 1876, which met at Cincinnati, he
nominated James G. Blaine for the presidency, and a
new and wondrous star blazed in the oratorical skies.
Later he practiced law in Washington and New York,
giving much time to lecturing against orthodox reli-

gious beliefs, and becoming known as " the eloquent agnostic." He also lectured on Shakespeare and other literary subjects and was in wide demand as a speaker on great occasions of historical or political nature. Wherever he spoke cheering crowds packed the hall or theater.

On the platform not even Webster looked more completely the orator than did this agnostic with the golden tongue. A large man, of regal bearing, he was always faultlessly attired; his face was full and round, forehead high, lips full and mobile above a dimpled chin. His eyes were bright and capable of flashing scorn or signaling sympathy. Graceful and at ease on the platform, his flights of fancy were such as to magnetize his hearers, yet withal there was an undertone of sadness — akin to the melancholy days of late autumn with fading flowers and falling leaves. The word " exuberance " best describes the Ingersoll style. He thought in images, and no other American orator so loved and used " apt alliteration's artful aid." He possessed the poet's sensitiveness to words, the painter's to color, the musician's to harmony.

Although Ingersoll spoke with the tongue of an angel, his political speeches were often marred by extreme partisanship and the waving of the " bloody shirt." A one-time Democrat, he turned his heavy artillery on his former party and shelled the enemy remorselessly: " Every Democrat is not a horse thief," he declared, but " every horse thief is a Democrat. . . . Every man who is a Democrat is a Democrat because he hates something; every man who is a Republican is a Republican because he loves something. Democracy of the modern kind is built upon envy, upon hatred, upon ignorance, and upon treason. Republicanism is built upon love of liberty, upon a love of justice, upon a love of country, and upon the highest, the holiest and the noblest aspirations of the human heart." These are but a few samples of the vials of vitriol he poured upon the party of Jefferson, attacks so biased that their very extravagance made them slightly ludicrous.

In his attacks on religion, Ingersoll smote many a theological vagary hip and thigh, and his frontal attack on extreme Calvinism — the dogmas of hell-fire and infant damnation — was scorching. In his own way he probably did the cause of religious truth a real service, although he often failed to differentiate between what was temporary and transient, and the permanent principles of both Judaism and Christianity. He cracked the shell of forms, ceremonies, extreme and fanatical theories, but the wholesome kernel of real religion suffered not at all. He enjoyed poking fun at the preachers. " I would rather smoke one cigar than to hear two sermons," he wrote; yet Thomas Dixon, Jr., the well known Baptist preacher and author, probably spoke for a multitude of Christians when in a statement frankly disagreeing with the colonel he said: " Ingersoll stabbed to the heart hundreds of superstitions and lies that have been no part of vital Christianity, and yet have passed as divine truth. He has done much to rid the world of the superstitions, lies, shams, humbugs and pretense that pass current as orthodox truth."

Ingersoll's national fame was achieved by his speech nominating Blaine at Cincinnati in 1876, an amazing performance. The speech was brief, not over ten minutes, and one of the most remarkable in the annals of American political conventions. There follows the famous excerpt which set the convention in a frenzy of cheering:

Like an armed warrior, like a plumed knight, James G. Blaine marched down the halls of the American Congress and threw his shining lances full and fair against the brazen foreheads of every defamer of his country and maligner of its honor.

For the Republican party to desert a gallant man now is worse than if an army should desert their general upon the field of battle. . . .

Gentlemen of the convention, in the name of the great republic, the only republic that ever existed upon this earth; in the name of all her defenders and of all her supporters; in the name of all her soldiers living; in the name of all her soldiers who died upon the field of battle; and in the name of those who perished in the skeleton clutch of famine at Andersonville and Libby, whose sufferings he so eloquently remembers, Illinois nominates for the next president of this country that prince of parliamentarians, that leader of leaders — James G. Blaine.

Colonel Ingersoll excelled in vivid descriptive passages. Here his style was pictorial, kaleidoscopic, panoramic. A paragraph from his speech delivered at Indianapolis in 1876 to the veterans of the war only a decade past, shows him at his best. Imagine the effect of these vivid pictures passing in swift procession before the people, pictures painted by a master with the skill of a Raphael or a Titian.

The past rises before me like a dream. Again we are in the great struggle for national life. We hear the sounds of preparation; the music of boisterous drums; the silver voices of heroic bugles. We see thousands of assemblages and hear the appeals of orators. We see the pale cheeks of women, and the flushed faces of men; and in those assemblages we see all the dead whose dust we have covered with flowers. We lose sight of them no more. We are with them when they enlist in the great army of freedom. We see them part with those they love. Some are walking for the last time in quiet, woody places with the maidens they adore. We hear the whisperings and the sweet vows of eternal love as they lingeringly part forever. Others are bending over cradles, kissing babes that are asleep. Some are receiving the blessings of old men. Some are parting with mothers who hold them and press them to their hearts again and again and say nothing. Kisses and tears, tears and kisses — divine mingling of agony and love! And some are talking with wives, and endeavoring with brave words, spoken in the old tones, to drive from their hearts the awful fear. We see them part. We see the wife standing in the door with the babe in her arms — standing in the sunlight, sobbing. At the turn in the road a hand waves — she answers by holding high in her loving arms the child. He is gone, and forever!

Colonel Ingersoll was devoted to the opera, and to grand opera most of all. Wagner was his favorite, and he considered Anton Seidl " the noblest, tenderest, and the most artistic interpreter of Wagner who had ever lived." When Seidl died, Ingersoll was in Wheeling, West Virginia, and was unable to attend the funeral. He sent a telegram to be read on that occasion. And such a telegram it was! Surely never before that date (March 30, 1898) , or since, has there been sent over the wires such a rapturous eulogy.

In the noon and zenith of his career, in the flush and glory of success, Anton Seidl, the greatest orchestral leader of all time, the perfect interpreter of Wagner, of all his subtlety and sympathy, his heroism and grandeur, his intensity and limitless passion, his wondrous harmonies that tell of all there is in life, and touch the longings and the hopes of every heart, has passed from the shores of sound to the realm of silence, borne by the mysterious and resistless tide that ever ebbs but never flows.

All moods were his. Delicate as the perfume of the first violet, wild as the storm, he knew the music of all sounds, from the rustle of leaves, the whisper of hidden springs, to the voices of the sea.

He was the master of music, from the rhythmical strains of irresponsible joy to the sob of the funeral march.

He stood like a king with his scepter in his hand, and we knew that every tone and harmony were in his brain, every passion in his breast, and yet his sculptured face was as calm, as serene as perfect art. He mingled his soul with the music and gave his heart to the enchanted air.

He appeared to have no limitations, no walls, no chains. He seemed to follow the pathway of desire, and the marvelous melodies, the sublime harmonies, were as free as eagles above the clouds with outstretched wings.

He educated, refined, and gave unspeakable joy to many thousands of his fellow men. He added to the grace and glory of life. He spoke a language deeper, more poetic than words — the language of the perfect, the language of love and death.

But he is voiceless now; a fountain of harmony has ceased. Its inspired strains have died away in night, and all its murmuring melodies are strangely still.

We will mourn for him, we will honor him, not in words, but in the language that he used.

Anton Seidl is dead. Play the great funeral march. Envelop him in music. Let its wailing waves cover him. Let its wild and mournful winds sigh and moan above him. Give his face to its kisses and its tears.

Play the great funeral march, music as profound as death.
That will express our sorrow — that will voice our love, our
hope, and that will tell of the life, the triumph, the genius, the
death of Anton Seidl.

This orator was a lover of poetry and the drama.   He
admired Shakespeare extravagantly, and Robert Burns
was one of his heroes.   The last time that he visited
Scotland, and while he was sojourning at the birthplace
of Burns, he wrote the poem with which he was accustomed to conclude his lectures on the Scottish bard.   An
autographed copy of this poem may be seen framed and
hanging on the wall of that humble cottage where
Robert Burns first saw the light of day.

> Though Scotland boasts a thousand names
>   Of patriot, king and peer,
> The noblest, grandest of them all
>   Was loved and cradled here;
> Here lived the gentle peasant-prince
>   The loving cotter-king,
> Compared with whom the greatest lord
>   Is but a titled thing.
>
> 'Tis but a cot roofed in with straw,
>   A hovel made of clay;
> One door shuts out the snow and storm,
>   One window greets the day;
> And yet I stand within this room
>   And hold all thrones in scorn;
> For here, beneath this lowly thatch,
>   Love's sweetest bard was born.
>
> Within this hallowed hut I feel
>   Like one who clasps a shrine,
> When the glad lips at last have touched
>   The something deemed divine,

> And here the world through all the years,
>   As long as day returns,
> The tribute of its love and tears
>   Will pay to Robert Burns.

The most rewarding of all the Ingersoll lectures was the one on Shakespeare. This wizard of words had made a life study of the poet and in two hours of copious oratory poured out in brilliant profusion his encyclopedic knowledge, apt quotations, lucid interpretations, making the rather dim figure of the myriad-minded poet live again. In a glorious paragraph he closes this finest of his lectures:

> Shakespeare was an intellectual ocean whose waves touched all the shores of thought; within which were all the tides and waves of destiny and will; over which swept all the storms of fate, ambition and revenge; upon which fell the gloom and darkness of despair and death, and all the sunlight of content and love, and within which was the inverted sky lit with the eternal stars — an intellectual ocean — toward which all rivers ran, and from which now the isles and continents of thought receive their dew and rain.

No summary of this orator would be complete that did not include his splendid soliloquy at the grave of Napoleon Bonaparte. As he contemplated the " magnificent tomb of gilt and gold " and " gazed upon the sarcophagus of rare and nameless marble " he was moved to utter this sentiment:

> I thought of the orphans and widows he had made — of the tears that had been shed for his glory, and of the only woman who ever loved him — pushed from his heart by the cold hand of ambition. And I said, I would rather have been a French

peasant and worn wooden shoes. I would rather have lived in a hut with a vine growing over the door, and the grapes growing purple in the amorous kisses of the autumn sun. I would rather have been that poor peasant, with my loving wife by my side, knitting as the day died out of the sky — with my children upon my knees and their arms about me — I would rather have been that man, and gone down to the tongueless silence of the dreamless dust than to have been that imperial impersonation of force and murder known as Napoleon the Great.

Ingersoll's lecture on Abraham Lincoln is ranked with the few noble eulogies which deserve to live. It is a combination of short terse sentences with an occasional long and involved periodic phrasing filling an entire paragraph. His contrasting of the two speeches of Gettysburg, Everett's and Lincoln's, is exceptionally strong:

If you wish to know the difference between an orator and an elocutionist — between what is felt and what is said — between what the heart and brain can do together, and what the brain can do alone — read Lincoln's wondrous speech at Gettysburg, and then the oration of Edward Everett. The speech of Lincoln will never be forgotten. It will live until languages are dead and lips are dust. The oration of Everett will never be read.

The elocutionists believe in the virtue of voice, the sublimity of syntax, the majesty of long sentences, and the genius of gesture. The orator loves the real, the simple, the natural. He places the thought above all. He knows the greatest ideas should be expressed in the shortest words — that the greatest statues need the least drapery.

In harmony with this appraisal of real oratory, Colonel Ingersoll brings his own tribute to Lincoln to a close in simplest fashion:

" He spoke not to blame, not to upbraid, but to convince. He raised his hands, not to strike, but in benediction.

" He longed to pardon.

" He loved to see the pearls of joy on the cheeks of a wife whose husband he had rescued from death.

" Lincoln was the grandest figure of the fiercest civil war. He is the gentlest memory of our world."

This is effective speech-making, and charms by its simplicity, but does it quite measure up to this tribute by Homer Hoch, Kansas congressman, delivered in the national House of Representatives February 12, 1923:

There is no new thing to be said of Lincoln. There is no new thing to be said of the mountains, or of the sea, or of the stars. The years go their way, but the same old mountains lift their granite shoulders above the drifting clouds; the same mysterious sea beats upon the shore; and the same silent stars keep holy vigil above a tired world. But to mountains and sea and stars men turn forever in unwearied homage. And thus with Lincoln. For he was mountain in grandeur of soul, he was sea in deep undervoice of mystic loneliness, he was star in steadfast purity of purpose and of service. And he abides.

The most widely known speech of Ingersoll's and the one upon which his fame rests secure is his address at the grave of his brother, Ebon C. Ingersoll, who was a member of Congress and died at Washington. These brothers loved each other with a very great love, and the death of Ebon came to Robert as a devastating blow. One of the pallbearers appointed by the House of Representatives was Adlai E. Stevenson of Illinois, former vice-president of the United States. Mr. Stevenson was my neighbor for many years in Bloomington, and his description of the funeral and of Colonel Ingersoll's address, as he related it to me, was most impressive. He said that as the cortege reached the cemetery a gentle rain began to fall, and at the grave-side, standing in the pattering drops, Colonel Ingersoll drew from his coat pocket a manuscript, and spoke in a voice trembling with emotion:

Dear Friends: I am going to do that which the dead oft promised he would do for me.

The loved and loving brother, husband, father, friend, died where manhood's morning almost touches noon, and while the shadows still were falling toward the west.

He had not passed on life's highway the stone that marks the highest point, but, being weary for a moment, lay down by the wayside, and, using his burden for a pillow, fell into that dreamless sleep that kisses down his eyelids still. While yet in love with life and raptured with the world, he passed to silence and pathetic dust.

Yet, after all, it may be best, just in the happiest, sunniest hour of all the voyage, while eager winds are kissing every sail, to dash against the unseen rock, and in an instant hear the billows roar above a sunken ship. For, whether in mid-sea or 'mong the breakers of the farther shore, a wreck at last must mark the end of each and all. And every life, no matter if its every hour is rich with love and every moment jeweled with a joy, will, at its close, become a tragedy as sad and deep and dark as can be woven of the warp and woof of mystery and death.

This brave and tender man in every storm of life was oak and rock, but in the sunshine he was vine and flower. He was the friend of all heroic souls. He climbed the heights and left all superstitions far below, while on his forehead fell the golden dawning of the grander day.

He loved the beautiful, and was with color, form and music touched to tears. He sided with the weak, and with a willing hand gave alms; with loyal heart and with purest hands he faithfully discharged all public trusts.

He was a worshiper of liberty, a friend of the oppressed. A thousand times I have heard him quote these words: " For justice all place a temple, and all seasons, summer." He believed that happiness was the only good, reason the only torch, justice the only worship, humanity the only religion, and love the only priest.

He added to the sum of human joy; and were everyone to whom he did some loving service to bring a blossom to his grave, he would sleep tonight beneath a wilderness of flowers.

Life is a narrow vale between the cold and barren peaks of two eternities. We strive in vain to look beyond the heights. We cry aloud, and the only answer is the echo of our wailing cry. From the voiceless lips of the unreplying dead there comes no word; but in the night of death hope sees a star, and listening love can hear the rustle of a wing.

He who sleeps here, when dying, mistaking the approach of death for the return of health, whispered with his last breath: " I am better now." Let us believe, in spite of doubts and dogmas, and tears and fears, that these dear words are true of all the countless dead.

And now to you who have been chosen, from among the many men he loved, to do the last sad office for the dead, we give his sacred dust. Speech cannot contain our love. There was, there is, no greater, stronger, manlier man.*

Here again are the hallmarks of the greatest oratorical triumphs: a theme of universal interest and appeal; brevity, deep pathos combined with lovely imagery, and the sheer artistry of short sentences inter-

* Text as printed in the *New York Tribune,* June 4, 1879, and quoted in *The World's Famous Orations,* Vol. X.

woven with the longer forms. Add to this the confession of faith bursting through the wall of doubt as the setting sun bursts through storm clouds, flooding the landscape with ethereal beauty, and the effect is perfect. If Robert G. Ingersoll had pronounced only this tribute, at once so beautiful and so sad, it would have been enough to number him among those who spoke with the tongues of angels.

THE BRECKINRIDGES

Born to the Oratorical Purple

THE BRECKINRIDGES

THE REMARKABLE Breckinridge family traces through remote root to John Knox, reformer of Scotland, and to the Breckinridges and Hopkins' of England; more directly to Dr. John Witherspoon and the Smiths of Princeton, New Jersey; and to the Breckinridges, Cabells and Prestons, first families of Virginia. The founder of the Kentucky branch was John Breckinridge, eldest son of Colonel Robert Breckinridge of Augusta county, Virginia. Educated at William and Mary, John married Mary Hopkins Cabell of Virginia and after a brief and brilliant beginning in the Old Dominion moved to Kentucky, where he became one of her most distinguished citizens and a staunch supporter of Thomas Jefferson. He served in the United States Senate and was attorney general in President Jefferson's second administration.

The Kentucky Breckinridges were orators, fighters, statesmen, Presbyterian clergymen, independent thinkers. The Breckinridge men were big and handsome, the women capable and intelligent. The family divided during the war between the states and their brains, eloquence and social influence were employed almost equally for and against the union. The eloquent and scholarly Dr. Robert J. went with the union, the handsome and eloquent John C. with the south, while two of R. J.'s sons fought in the southern army and two for the north.

John Breckinridge, founder of the Kentucky family, was a noble specimen of manhood, standing over six feet in height, with broad shoulders, brown eyes, and hair of a rich chestnut shade. A lawyer of exceptional ability, he stood at the head of the Lexington bar, was attorney general of Kentucky and speaker of the legislature in that state. He built his home a few miles from Lexington, near the Elkhorn creek, and named it "Cabell's Dale" for his young and beautiful wife. To the left of the house, on one corner of the lawn, he erected his law office, and for years this country place was a center of generous hospitality. President Jefferson had no more able and trusted lieutenant in the south than this gifted man, who was the author of the "Kentucky Resolutions" and a fervent advocate of Jeffersonian principles and policies. He died in 1806 in the maturity of his mental and physical vigor, an ornament to his profession and a statesman of first-class mind and great natural gifts.

Of the able sons of John Breckinridge the most illustrious in point of influence, intellect and noble character was Robert J., born in 1800. A Presbyterian clergyman of distinction, a persuasive orator and the master of a trenchant pen, opposer of slavery and stalwart supporter of the union, he was one of the potent personalities who prevented Kentucky from joining the Confederacy. The fact that his own flesh and blood, together with many of his dearest friends, were on the other side of the burning issue did not deter him in the smallest degree. Upon this heroic man Abraham Lincoln leaned heavily, greatly prizing his friendship.

In appearance Breckinridge was tall and spare, though big of frame. His beard was iron gray at the sides and snowy white beneath his chin. He wore steel spectacles, behind which his keen eyes flashed with fire and conviction. His character was such as to command the respect of his bitterest political enemies, and the weight of a great family name reinforced the influence of his logic and the splendor of his speech.

As the editor of the *Quarterly Review*, Breckinridge reached multitudes who were unable to hear his public addresses, and wherever he spoke crowds struggled to gain admittance to the hall or church. His crowning service for the union was his speech as temporary chairman of the Baltimore convention which renominated Lincoln. In the course of that speech he lifted himself far above mere partisan politics when he declared:

As a union party I will follow you to the end of the earth and to the gates of death. But as an abolition party, as a Republican party, as a Whig party, as a Democratic party, as an American party, I will not follow you one foot. . . . I know very well that the sentiments I am uttering will cause a great odium in the state in which I was born, which I love, where the bones of two generations of my ancestors and some of my children are, and where very soon I shall lay my own. I know very well that my colleagues will incur odium if they endorse what I say and they, too, know it. But [and he raised his arms high above his head and spoke with a firm, slow, ringing emphasis] we have put our faces toward the way in which we intend to go, and we will go in it to the end.

The day following this speech Breckinridge was in Washington with the committee to notify Lincoln of his nomination, and on Sunday, June 12, he preached in the Hall of Representatives " a pure gospel sermon and very able." So wrote one who was present on that notable occasion. A rare man and of leonine courage was this preacher-orator, Robert J. Breckinridge, who finished his course in 1871.

Equally brilliant and of even superior oratorical gifts, but much more the man of the world, was the old doctor's nephew, John C. Breckinridge, one of the most fascinating, dashing and lovable of all southerners. Of a family of handsome men he was perhaps the handsomest. He was the Chevalier Bayard type with hair dark and abundant, large eloquent eyes, a firm and beautiful mouth, small hands and feet. Meticulous as to dress and a natural showman, his platform presence was singularly impressive. Brady's daguerreotype of John C., made when he was vice-president, resembles the pictures of President Franklin Pierce, but the mouth is more oratorical and the head held even more regally.

Admired by Abraham Lincoln, who called him " John "; ranked by James G. Blaine as the most promising and popular of southern statesmen; idolized by his friends and followers — John C. was quick to notice a slight or resent an insult. In politics at twenty-three, in Congress at thirty, vice-president at thirty-five,

impetuous and lovable, proud and generous, arrogant
and friendly, John C. Breckinridge was a medley of
contradictions which only added piquancy to his personality. His father was Joseph Cabell Breckinridge
who, though he died at the age of thirty-five, had been
a representative in the Kentucky legislature and
speaker of the House and was secretary of state for
Governor John Adair at the time of his death. John C.
was born January 15, 1821, at Cabell's Dale, ancestral
home of his father, and educated at Pisgah Academy in
Woodford county, Centre College, Danville, and at the
College of New Jersey. He studied law under the direction of Governor William Owsley, and completed
his law studies at Transylvania University. Forming a
law partnership in Lexington, his rise in his profession
and in politics was meteoric.

There are grounds for believing that the two most
brilliant and promising men in the American political
scene, who dazzled their generations only to go into
eclipse, were Aaron Burr of New York and John C.
Breckinridge of Kentucky. Both served as vice-president of the United States, Burr missing the presidency
by a single vote, while Breckinridge as a presidential
candidate in the four-cornered contest of 1860, received the second largest electoral vote, though falling
behind Stephen A. Douglas in the popular ballot. No
one knows how far Burr might have gone had he not
slain Colonel Hamilton in the tragic duel and strangely
involved himself in mysterious alliances which cast
doubts on his loyalty; nor can anyone say what John C.
Breckinridge might not have enjoyed at the hands of

his fellow citizens had he restrained his impetuous nature and espoused the cause of the union in the fateful years of the fratricidal war. After the manner of Robert E. Lee of Arlington, John C. Breckinridge believed his allegiance belonged to the south and to the cause of the Confederacy, which he espoused with lavish devotion; he saw much action, serving as a major general, and for a brief period toward the end of the conflict as President Davis' secretary of war.

A study of John C. Breckinridge's published speeches, coupled with contemporary judgment, seems to warrant the conclusion that he was oratorically the most accomplished of the family, though there is room for difference of opinion here. His style was classical and restrained, chaste and polished, unembarrassed by floridity. His eulogy in the House of Representatives on the passing of Henry Clay was a jewel; and the address he delivered on the occasion of the removal of the United States Senate to their new chamber was a majestic piece of rhetoric. There follows from the last-named address the paragraph devoted to the Great Triumvirate:

There sat Calhoun, the senator, inflexible, austere, oppressed, but not overwhelmed by his deep sense of the importance of his public functions, seeking the truth, then fearlessly following it — a man whose unsparing intellect compelled all his notions to harmonize with deductions of his rigorous logic and whose noble countenance habitually wore the expression of one engaged in the performance of high public duties.

This was Webster's seat. He, too, was every inch a senator. Conscious of his own vast powers, he reposed with confidence in himself, and, scorning the contrivances of smaller men, he stood among his peers all the greater for the simple dignity of

his senatorial demeanor. Type of his northern home, he rises
before the imagination, in the grand and granite outline of his
form and intellect, like a great New England rock, repelling a
New England wave. As a senatorial orator, his great efforts
are historically associated with this chamber, whose very air
seems to vibrate beneath the strokes of his deep tones and his
weighty words.

On the outer circle sat Henry Clay, with his impetuous and
ardent nature untamed by age and exhibiting in the Senate the
same vehement patriotism and passionate eloquence that of
yore electrified the House of Representatives and the country.
His extraordinary personal endowments, his courage, all his
noble qualities, invested him with an individuality and a
charm of character which in any age would have made him a
favorite of history. He loved his country above all earthly ob-
jects. He loved liberty in all countries. Illustrious man! Orator, patriot, philanthropist, whose light, at its meridian, was
seen and felt in the remotest parts of the civilized world, and
whose declining sun, as it hastened down the west, threw back
its level beams in hues of mellowed splendor to illuminate and
to cheer the land he loved and served so well.

And now, senators, we leave this memorable chamber, bearing with us unimpaired the Constitution we received from our
forefathers. Let us cherish it with grateful acknowledgments
to the divine Power who controls the destinies of empires and
whose goodness we adore. The structures reared by men yield
to the corroding tooth of time. These marble walls must
molder into ruin, but the principles of constitutional liberty,
guarded by wisdom and virtue, unlike material elements, do
not decay. Let us devoutly trust that another Senate, in another age, shall bear to a new and larger chamber this Constitution, vigorous and inviolate, and that the last generation of
posterity shall witness the deliberations of the representatives
of American states still united, prosperous and free.

The effect of John's eloquence upon those who listened spellbound to his flights is described in James

Tandy Ellis' poem, "The Old Elm Tree Where Breckinridge Spoke." The verses give in the vernacular of a plain farmer his recollection of the famous event. There are eighteen stanzas, of which three are reproduced here:

> Well, after we had gotten through
> A-messin' at the barbecue
> We gethered round that tree,
> The men and women left the creek
> For they had come to hear him speak —
> The great John C.
>
> .   .   .   .
>
> He took us back to Washington,
> John Adams and old Jefferson,
> And told us of the worth
> Of these old statesmen, then he led
> Us to the very fountainhead
> Of Democratic birth.
>
> .   .   .   .
>
> If there be orators in heaven
> When I git thar and I am given
> A chance to hear them speak,
> I'm going to say to old John C.,
> " Jest say agin that speech for me
> You made on Eagle creek."

Following the collapse of the Confederacy General Breckinridge, who was one of the last important commanders to surrender, spent several years of exile in Europe and Canada. In 1868 President Andrew Johnson issued a proclamation of amnesty to the people of Kentucky, and in March, 1869, John C. returned to his beloved Lexington. Coming from Cincinnati by train he was greeted by cheering crowds at the stations along the way and by an outpouring of old friends and admirers at Lexington. But the fire had gone out of the man; his heart was in the grave of the Confederacy. He held himself proudly, though broken in spirit and suffering from an incurable malady. Never asking and never receiving the right of citizenship, he made a few cautious speeches, turned his interest to the development of transportation, became vice-president of the Lexington, Elizabethtown and Big Sandy Railroad, and devoted himself to business. But the untimely end was drawing near. In May, 1875, the general underwent a surgical operation from which he did not recover. Amid tears Lexington buried her hero with elaborate military and civic honors, and a decade later erected his statue on Cheapside Square. There his heroic-sized bronze image in the proud posture of an orator addressing an assembly looks calmly down on the scene where in the days of his flesh he was a dominant and thrilling figure.

The third oratorical member of this illustrious family was Colonel William Cabell Preston Breckinridge, one of the two sons of Robert J. who fought for the Confederacy. Widely heralded as "the silver-tongued orator of the south," member of Congress from the old " Ashland " district, the colonel was a lawyer of renown, and as editor of the *Lexington Herald* his picturesque editorials were as readily recognized as were those of Colonel Henry Watterson in the *Louisville Courier-Journal*.

The colonel's oratorical gifts were lavish: a soft musical voice, flexible and sweet, an opulent imagination, a fluency that beguiled while it charmed, and a manner of shaking his head which set his great white mane in motion as though it were beating time to the rhythmical speech. One of his feminine admirers declared it was worth going a hundred miles just to hear him pronounce the word "watah," and a masculine idolator held that he could put more into the phrase "the Democratic pahty" than most orators could put into an hour's speech. Extravagant of course, but revealing. William was especially effective in eulogistic or memorial addresses, when his solemn, tearful tones played dirges on the heartstrings of his hearers. It is related that Thomas B. Reed, then speaker of the House of Representatives, coming into the hall one day while the colonel was speaking in tristful cadences, stopped, listened, and inquired: "Who's dead now?"

It was my privilege to hear this distinguished orator during my student days in Transylvania, 1897–1900, and the music of his mellifluous voice still lingers in my memory. In common with all the Breckinridge men Colonel W. C. P. was broad-shouldered, and his noble head was crowned with a great shock of graying hair, one lock of which hung over his right eye. Unlike his illustrious father, he wore his beard closely cropped, and in place of his sire's tall, slender frame, the colonel's build was heavy-set and not much above the average height. As I observed him on the streets of Lexington he usually carried a handkerchief in his right hand and wore a soft bell-crowned hat, which he constantly lifted in response to numerous salutations. To the end of his days the colonel walked the streets of his native town lifting his hat and bowing low, a courtly gentleman of the old school.

A speech at Hopkinsville, Kentucky, May 19, 1887, "Who Were the Confederate Dead?" is memorable. Here are two paragraphs:

In the presence of this sad assemblage, in the presence of the dead, in the sight of God, I feel that it would be sacrilege to utter one word that is not in every sense true. With this solemn thought pressing upon me, I believe that I utter the sentiment of those who hear me when I say that we trust the day may come when such peace will bless our land that all the living will lovingly do honor to all the dead. We are all Americans, we are citizens of a common country in whose destinies are involved the destinies of our children. Around us in this cemetery lie buried the dead of all. Religion, patriotism, the love we bear our children, alike appeal with eloquent earnestness for the return of good feeling and brotherly love.

At the foot of this stately monument of granite, this stone hewn from the mountains of Maine, now planted in the heart of Kentucky in honor of soldiers from states so distant as Texas, we pray God to grant that in that ceaseless contest our children may be as heroic, as enduring, as pure as these unknown dead, ready to live for the right, willing, if need be, to die for the right, as God gives it to them to see the right.

Once I was fortunate enough to hear Colonel Breckinridge speak for two hours on the Constitution, and such an oratorical treat I never expect to enjoy again. He pronounced it "constichution," with the emphasis on the "chu." He sketched with broad strokes the historical background; limned with delicate touch vignettes of the leaders — Hamilton, Madison,

Mason; analyzed the document with artistry and skill. As he wound to a close he threw back his great head, shook his gray mane, and said:

There are those among us who talk about the great old days as though there would never be other great days. I cannot agree with these croaking pessimists. As for myself I en-vy the boys and girls playing in the streets of Lex-ing-ton, for they will see gr-eat-er and gr-an-der things than their forefathers ever dr-eam-ed of — mar-ve-lous triumphs, un-pre-dictable achievè-ments, not even the e-ter-nal God has set limits to the bound-a-ries of our mi-igh-ty republic.

It was not so much what he said as the way he said it — the sweet beguiling voice, the limpid flow of sentences, some long and involved, others short and terse, while the great white mane flopping up and down imparted to the speaker a picturesqueness which was tremendously effective.

The colonel was in political eclipse at this time, following the sensational trial in which he was defendant — a trial that rocked the nation and set Kentucky agog. Despite the furor caused by the scandal he attempted a political comeback and announced his candidacy for the nomination to his old congressional seat. It was the livest sort of campaign, since the two men who contested the nomination with Colonel Breckinridge were also spellbinders. Crowds came to hear the colonel. who was never more eloquent, or more contrite. But in vain. Many of his old friends refused him support and took the stump against him; the churches and preachers protested his nomination to the end. But he fought on, pleading. cajoling. appealing for another chance. " I have sinned," he said as only he could say it, " and I repent in sackcloth and ashes." The pathos was real, not simulated.

At the height of this spectacular campaign Charles C. Moore, the eccentric editor of the *Bluegrass Blade,* a self-styled " atheist " and the possessor of a racy literary style steeped in the classics, came to Breckinridge's defense in an editorial that was the talk of the town for months. I reproduce it from memory:

I have sympathy for Adam led astray by all the newborn beauty of the blushing Eve; I have sympathy for Acteon changed into a stag and hunted by his own hounds for gazing on the bathing Diana; I have sympathy for peeping Tom who gave his eyes for one look at the naked Lady Godiva; I have sympathy for Leander who swam the Hellespont to keep an engagement with his lovely Hero; I have sympathy for Henry Ward Beecher who tumbled to the racket of Bessie Tilton; and last, but not least, I have sympathy for Colonel William C. P. Breckinridge, scion of a famous Kentucky lineage, who dissolved his family pearls in wine at the shrine of a brilliant Kentucky woman and in mad intoxication drank the cup to its dregs. But may my right hand forget its cunning and my tongue cleave to the roof of my mouth if I ever write or speak one word in defense of the man who spends his nights in the gambling hells of Lexington and Louisville and then poses as a moralist by blasting Billy Breckinridge.

But despite his ardent campaign and some friends' support Colonel Breckinridge went down to defeat. With his death in 1904 there passed from Lexington an arresting personage and the last of the silver-tongued Breckinridges. Shortly after his death the Fayette county bar met in memorial session and John R. Allen, a long-time friend of the colonel's, delivered a eulogy of rare beauty, closing with this apostrophe:

Oh, brilliant and incomparable Breckinridge! We lay for a season thy precious dust beneath the soil that bore and cherished thee, but we fling back against our brightening skies the thoughtless speech that calls thee dead. God reigns, and his purpose lives, and although these brave lips are silent here, the seeds sown by this incarnate eloquence will sprinkle patriots through the years to come, and perpetuate thy living in a race of nobler men.

An eloquent tribute to an eloquent son of that section of America where " they grow orators."

PHILLIPS BROOKS

He Spoke as God's Ambassador

PHILLIPS BROOKS

LONG AGO a spiritual seer wrote, " Though I speak with the tongues of men and of angels, and have not love, I am become as sounding brass and a tinkling cymbal." This is a good warning for the oratorically minded, who need to read these words daily and ponder them deeply. A great speaker whose life subtracts from his words is of all men most pitiable. One recalls Emerson's, " How can I hear what you say when what you do keeps thundering in my ears? "

The glory of Phillips Brooks' life was not merely the fact that he thrilled men and women with his eloquence but that he inspired them to think nobly and act nobly. People came away from hearing him, exclaiming not " What a great orator! " but " What a great soul! " They did not say, " How he thrilled me! " but rather, " He made me think well of God." Henry Ward Beecher after listening to a sermon by Phillips Brooks is said to have remarked, " I'll never go into the pulpit again " — a characteristic speech by one who in sheer bravura and literary charm was Brooks' superior, yet recognized the inherent greatness of his contemporary and paid it homage.

Phillips Brooks sprang from fine old New England stock, cultured and religious. He was a lineal descendant of John Cotton, the famous divine, and on his father's side the stream of religion, education and public service was signally deep and fruitful. Born in Boston, December 13, 1835, young Brooks was carefully trained, first in private schools, then in the Boston Latin School and at Harvard, graduating from the latter at the age of nineteen. He taught for a brief period in the Latin School, decided to enter the ministry and matriculated in the seminary of the Protestant Episcopal Church at Alexandria, Virginia. There he made a reputation for sound scholarship and began the notebook habit, which he continued through all his happy, crowded years. He served as rector of the Church of the Advent, Philadelphia, for three years, and of Holy Trinity in the same city for seven years, making a notable impression and winning a large following. In 1869 he became rector of Trinity Church, Boston, where his ministry won international renown. In 1891 he was consecrated bishop of Massachusetts, serving until his death in 1893.

The eloquence of Phillips Brooks is inseparable not only from his beautiful character, but also from his liberal theology and the unique position he held in the Episcopal Church. In studying the background of Brooks the following excerpt from the Right Reverend William Lawrence, who succeeded him as bishop of Massachusetts, is revealing:

The Puritans were dogmatic and mystic, of deep religious experience. Their descendants, weakening on the spiritual side, had broken into two parties, both over-rationalistic, one dogmatic, the other discarding all dogma. The people were yearning for spiritual food, but husks were plenty. In the simpler creed and spiritual traditions of the Episcopal Church was the foundation of a revival of faith, but the spiritual element for which the people hungered was often lacking. From Coleridge, Wordsworth, Maurice, Robertson, Tennyson and Bushnell a fresh light had broken; and the young preacher of New England, Phillips Brooks, first in Philadelphia, then in Boston, and later throughout the country, gathering in his great personality the mysticism and spiritual experiences of his forebears, and interpreting history and the creeds through the living power of Christ, brought to the people a fresh and living gospel.

The discoveries of science, the theory of evolution, opposed by many ecclesiastics, were seized by him as fresh revelations of God's truth. Reacting from the Puritan dogma of original sin, he preached that all men are the sons of God, redeemed by their grateful recognition of the life, sacrifice and resurrection of Jesus Christ. Of course he, like all forerunners, was distrusted by the conservatives and deemed a heretic by those who thought and talked in the ways of the fathers; but the people of his own generation, the young men and women, understood him, gathered about him, and followed him. No artifice of sensationalism, no mechanics of eloquence were his. He spoke naturally, with rapid, rushing eloquence, out of the abundance of his heart and experience.

From the beginning of his ministry Brooks was made much over, praised, flattered. His parents observed this with concern. Thus his mother wrote: " I am glad you are prospering so well in your church. I hope you will always be faithful and humble. Sometimes, I fear, Phillips, that the praises of your friends will make you proud, for you are human; but do not let it." His father was even more pointed in expressing his anxiety. He wrote: " You are in a dangerous situation for a young man, and I cannot help warning you of it. Keep your simplicity and your earnestness, above all your devotion to your Master's cause; and don't let these flattering demonstrations you see about you withdraw you from them. Keep on in the even tenor of your ways, so that when there is a lull in the excitement it will find you the same." Excellent advice, though Phillips Brooks probably needed it less than most mortals.

What was the equipment of Phillips Brooks for his extraordinary ministry? First, a giant stature. His biographer, A. V. G. Allen, says that he was so tall that on coming into a friend's home he would playfully place his hat on some tall bookcase, where anyone else would have to mount on steps to reach it, and sometimes in a spirit of fun he would light his cigar from a street lamp. Yet his proportions were such as to prevent any semblance of clumsiness. His head was large and noble, eyes large — lustrous, glorious eyes they were. His voice was sympathetic and strong, but he did not always have complete mastery of it; sometimes it failed him momentarily, as it did once when he was preaching for Dean Stanley in Westminster Abbey. His utterance, which was pronounced " throaty " by one critic, was rapid, torrential, and the despair of reporters. William Cleaver Wilkinson heard him and wrote:

The preacher, from the very first word, begins his sermon, usually read from a manuscript, at a prodigious rate of speed in utterance. The words hurry out as if the weight of the Atlantic were on the reservoir behind them to give the escaping current irresistible head. There is no letup, there could be no acceleration, to the rush of the torrent. You feel at first as if you never should be able to follow at such a breakneck pace. But you soon find yourself caught up and borne forward, as it were, without your following, on the mighty breast of the onrushing flood. What is more, presently you enjoy riding so fast. There is a kind of impartation and transformation of personal living force, by virtue of which you not only understand everything uttered, but with ease understand it, more swiftly than your wont. The novel experience is delightful.

Intellectually Brooks' equipment was basically good. To the heritage of culture he added a student's acquisitiveness, a scholar's discriminating balance, and a wide and intimate acquaintance with the best in history, poetry, fiction, philosophy and science. He was a close observer of persons and things, and his notebook habit enabled him to save the sands of gold which most of us permit to slip through our busy fingers. He had the capacity for mental concentration, and could think and write despite numerous interruptions and quite regardless of what was going on around him.

He had his eccentricities. His house was filled with myriad volumes, beautiful pictures and relics gathered from the ends of the earth. He was happy in the possession of the manuscript of a sermon preached by Dean Stanley at Trinity Church, a clay pipe used by Tennyson and given to him by the poet, the manuscript of a sermon by Frederick D. Maurice, marble busts of Coleridge and Kingsley, an image of Buddha from India, casts of the faces of Cromwell and Lincoln. His favorite color was red, and he loved books bound in red morocco. He was always reading when traveling; but having finished a book, strange to record, he threw it out of the car window. He loved children, took them on his knee, got down on the floor and frolicked with them, let them climb on his broad back.

As almost everybody knows, Phillips Brooks was a bachelor, and he admitted that it was the mistake of his life not to have married. More than once he said to intimate friends: " The trouble with you married men is that you think no one has been in love but yourselves; I know what love is; I have been in love myself." Does this confession suggest a hidden romance? So it seems, but not even his best biographer, other than the recording of this significant remark, so much as hints at such a possibility. The great bishop was often smitten with a sense of vast loneliness, yet he kept his optimism and ever turned a serene and smiling face toward a troubled world.

Brooks was methodical in his habits. It was his custom to rise at seven. He kept no office hours and insisted on seeing anyone who called. Making a sermon was with him almost a ritual; preaching a fine art; the ministry a noble quest. He was usually in bed by eleven. He loved to walk, and his great figure was a familiar sight on Boston's streets.

He was a statesman of the spiritual realm. Yet more than physical or mental resources was this man's depth of character — sincerity, nobility of thought and deed.

Oliver Wendell Holmes described him as " the ideal minister of the American gospel." Yet this description is inadequate — there was a *universal* quality in the man and his preaching.

Specimens of Bishop Brooks' eloquence lack, as do all published speeches and sermons, the personality that gave them birth and passion. Yet there remains something of the great man's power and spirit. When Henry Ward Beecher died, Brooks preached from the text, " He that overcometh shall inherit all things," and at the close of the sermon said:

I know that you are all thinking as I speak of the great soul that has passed away, of the great preacher — for he was the greatest preacher in America, and the greatest preacher means the greatest power in the land. To make a great preacher, two things are necessary, the love of truth and the love of souls; and surely no man had greater love of truth or love of souls than Henry Ward Beecher. Great services, too, did he render to theology, which is making great progress now. It is not that we are discovering new truths, but that what lay dead and dry in men's souls has awakened. The Spirit of the Lord has been poured into humanity, and no one more than Mr. Beecher has helped to this, pouring his great insight and sympathy and courage out upon the truths which God gave him to deliver. A great leader in the theological world, believing in the divine Christ and in eternal hope for mankind, foremost in every great work and in all progress, one of that noble band of men whose hands clutched the throat of slavery and never relaxed their hold till the last shackle fell off; inspiring men to war, speaking words of love and reconciliation when peace had come, standing by the poor and oppressed, bringing a slave girl into his pulpit and making his people pay her ransom. A true American like Webster, a great preacher, a great leader, a great patriot, a great man.

In his lectures on preaching, delivered at Yale in 1877, occurs this interesting paragraph:

Of oratory, and all the marvelous mysterious ways of those who teach it, I dare say nothing. I believe in the true elocution teacher, as I believe in the existence of Halley's comet, which comes into sight of this earth once in about sixty-six years. But whatever you may learn or unlearn from him to your advantage, the real power of your oratory must be your own intelligent delight in what you are doing. Let your pulpit be to you what his studio is to the artist, or his court to the lawyer, or his laboratory to the chemist, or the broad field with its bugles and banners to the soldier, only far more sacredly let your pulpit be this to you, and you have the power which is to all rules what the soul is to the body. You have enthusiasm which is the breath of life.

" Enthusiam " — how vastly Brooks possessed it, and with what infinite zest he threw himself into his ministry. His doubts he kept to himself, his faith he preached with a sincerity that was all-consuming and of transforming power. His temperament was sweetly and serenely sanguine. He once said that Christianity was to him " just a dear great Figure standing with outstretched arms," and he might have added, and probably did, " saying, ' Come unto me all ye who are weary and heavy laden.' "

Phillips Brooks' eulogy on the passing of Lincoln, while not so pictorial as Beecher's and lacking the latter's riotous imaginative qualities, is rightly ranked with the noblest utterances evoked by the tragic death of the Emancipator. Observe the analytical character of these thoughtful paragraphs. The style is not simple but complex, and while clear, is involved:

As to the moral and mental powers which distinguish him, all embraceable under this general description of clearness or truth, the most remarkable thing is the way in which they blend with one another, so that it is next to impossible to examine them in separation. A great many people have discussed very crudely whether Abraham Lincoln was an intellectual man or not; as if intellect were a thing always of the same sort, which you could precipitate from the other constituents of a man's nature and weigh by itself, and compare by pounds and ounces in this man with another. The fact is that in all the simplest characters the line between the mental and moral natures is always vague and indistinct. They run together, and in their best combination you are unable to discriminate, in the wisdom which is their result, how much is moral and how much is intellectual. You are unable to tell whether, in the wise acts and words which issue from such a life, there is more of the righteousness that comes of a clear conscience or of the sagacity that comes of a clear brain. In more complex characters and under more complex conditions the moral and mental lives come to be less healthily combined. They cooperate and help each other less. They come more to stand over against each other as antagonists; till we have that vague but melancholy notion which pervades the life of all elaborate civilization, that goodness and greatness, as we call them, are not to be looked for together; till we expect to see, and do see, a feeble and narrow conscientiousness on the one hand and a bad, unprincipled intelligence on the other, dividing the suffrages of men.

It is the great boon of such characters as Mr. Lincoln's that they reunite what God has joined together and what man has put asunder. In him was vindicated the greatness of real goodness and the goodness of real greatness. The twain were one flesh. Not one of all the multitudes who stood and looked up to him for direction, with such loving and implicit trust, can tell you today whether the wise judgments that he gave came most from a wise head or a sound heart. If you ask them they are puzzled. There are men as good as he, but they do bad things; there are men as intelligent as he, but they do foolish things. In him goodness and intelligence combined and made their best result of wisdom. For perfect truth consists not merely in the right constituents of character, but in their right and intimate conjunction. The union of the mental and moral into a life of admirable simplicity is what we most admire in children, but in them it is unsettled and unpractical. But when it is preserved into a manhood, deepened into reliability and maturity, it is that glorified childlikeness, that high and revered simplicity, which shames and baffles the most accomplished astuteness, and is chosen by God to fill his purposes when he needs a ruler for his people of faithful and true heart such as he had who was our President.

From a typical sermon on " How Many Loaves Have Ye? " this fine paragraph is taken. Mark the tolerant spirit of the man, his nice sense of justice and fairness:

To every man who has advanced or who hopes that he may advance to higher, fuller, truer views of Christian truth, I think that this lesson of the loaves has something very plain to say. I see a man who thinks differently today from the way in which he thought ten years ago. He knows more truth. He is sure that God has given him new knowledge. How shall that man look back to what he used to know, to his old creed? Surely he may, with all rejoicing for the fuller light to which he has been brought, own the half-light in which he used to walk, and honor it. He may remember with reverence how through some most imperfect conception of truth, which he could not possibly hold now, he came into the larger knowledge where he now finds his joy. Out of the notions which are dead now, he has drawn the life by which he lives. I think it is always a shame for a man to abuse any creed which, whatever was its power or its weakness, could do nothing for a man like him. If he was sincere, let him know that much of the good faith with which he holds his new dear truth comes from the training of that old devotion. No, if God has led you to see truth which once you did not see, and to reject as error what once you thought was true, do not try to signalize your new allegiance by defaming your old master. The man who thinks to make much of the fuller truth to which he has come by upbraiding the partial truth through which he came to it, is a poor creature. If I met a Mohammedan who had turned Christian, I would not like to hear him revile Mohammedanism. If I talk with a man from some other communion who has come into our church, I think the less and not the more of his churchmanship if he is always ready to defame the mother that bore him. If you are a more liberal believer than you used to be, the best proof that you can give of it will be in gratefully honoring the narrower creed in which you lived and by whose power you grew up and passed on.

Such preaching as this has in it an epic sweep and spiritual grandeur combined with a sweet reasonableness, and it is addressed to both the head and the heart. A scrutiny of these excerpts — save perhaps the last — shows clearly that this preeminent preacher was more concerned with the substance of his thought than with literary style. Some of the sentences are clumsy and occasionally there is an infelicity of phrasing such as one seldom, if ever, finds in Beecher's published sermons and orations. Indeed, Bishop Brooks never consciously delivered an " oration." He did not prune and polish his sermons; he wrote rapidly and his purpose was primarily not to say a thing well, but rather to impress his hearers with the truth which was upper-most in his mind. How different it was with, say, Inger-soll who, though no less engrossed with the views he advocated, loved the music of words, the rhythm of speech, and wrote and rewrote a sentence until it satis-fied his artistic nature. He used words as a painter mixes colors or as a musician searches for harmony. Brooks loved human beings more than words.

Phillips Brooks was assailed for his liberality, his orthodoxy was questioned. Whisperings about his heretical views filled the air, but they did not become vociferous until his election as bishop. Then the storm broke. What was the nature of this preacher's heresy? Here is an extract from a sermon that the ultra-con-servative held up as containing dangerous doctrine:

> We are His children, whether the best or the worst of us, those who are living the most upright lives, as well as those the most profligate, are all Christ's children. . . . Men are so commonly preached to that they are a great deal wickeder than they are, that they must not set so high worth upon hu-manity. I tell you we want another kind of preaching along with that. There is in every man something greater than he has begun to dream of. Men are nobler than they think them-selves. When a man gives himself in consecration to Jesus Christ, then that nobility comes forth until he shines like a star. *Go home and believe in yourselves more.*

Would Phillips Brooks be saying that if he lived to-day? I think he would.

When Phillips Brooks was in India it was announced that he would speak at Delhi, and the missionaries from all the provinces eagerly gathered there to hear him.

But the famous preacher did not appear, and the disappointment was keen. Some censured him, but those who knew him best were sure there was a good reason for his absence. And when the facts came out no one was critical of Phillips Brooks. This is what had happened: He was accompanied on the journey by a man who acted as his valet, although Brooks would not have so designated him. This man was stricken with smallpox, and the bishop canceled his engagements in order to devote himself to nursing his personal servant; nor did he leave the man's side until the disease had run its course. This incident is chronicled here not because it was unusual, but because it was characteristic of a man in whom resided the Spirit of the One he so gloriously preached.

Fifty-eight years of this noble man's life — years of incessant, busy ministry — preaching; lecturing; sitting in myriad conferences; writing innumerable letters; shepherding the suffering and succoring the needy; performing the sacraments of baptism, confirmation and marriage; traveling; administering the office of the episcopacy. A full life. And then, on January 23, 1893, the silver cord was loosed, the golden bowl broken. At his death Boston was stunned, the nation mourned, Christendom grieved, and messages from near and far poured in upon the bachelor home of a mighty prophet of the Most High.

On a late August afternoon I crossed the threshold of old Trinity Church, Boston. The structure was undergoing repairs, the workmen had finished their day's work and gone home. The grand old church seemed deserted. I entered and sat down in a pew five rows from the rear. Sitting there in the " dim religious light " I mused on Phillips Brooks, his life of faith and love. At first I thought I was the only person in the place, when I was startled by the sound of someone's sobbing. After my vision had grown accustomed to the semi-darkness, I saw a woman kneeling in prayer across the aisle four rows ahead of me. Her face was buried in her hands, which rested on the back of the pew in front of her; and as she sobbed her slender shoulders shook with emotion. In a little while she sat erect and wiped away her tears, arose and walked out of the church. As she passed by me a shaft of soft light brought out her fine strong profile; her head was thrown back, and on her face was a look of serene and lofty courage. I bowed my own head, and a little later as I left the place I said to myself, half aloud: " The spirit of Phillips Brooks still lives in this house of worship."

ALBERT J. BEVERIDGE

"Brilliant Beveridge" — *a superbly "made" Orator*

⚓XIII⚓

ALBERT J. BEVERIDGE

IF EVER A MAN won oratorical renown by constant practice and the most painstaking preparation, that man was Albert Jeremiah Beveridge of Indiana. He was a " boy orator " and the winner of numerous college prizes in public speaking, and managed to survive the handicap. He began his speaking early. In the year 1876, at work as a plow-boy on an Indiana farm, he was unable to forget the speech he had heard the night before by John A. Logan. At last he drove his team into a corner of the fence, and mounting a stump repeated as much of General Logan's speech as he could recall, delivering it to the skies, the fields, the trees, and his horses. The latter pricked up their ears as if entranced and swished their tails as if in applause — or so at any rate it seemed to the fourteen year old Cicero.

At DePauw University this oratorical fledgling tried his wings again and again, and always with success, since he wrote out his speeches with scrupulous care and committed them to memory. He " made " the swank Delta Kappa Epsilon fraternity, despite the fact that he was poor and without aristocratic social standing. His oratory and a certain proud demeanor set him apart. His serious, finely chiseled face and studious habits made him a marked man in the days when the literary society was considered more important than the athletic field.   An article he wrote on the ponderous theme " The Rise and Fall of Human Intelligence " was featured in the college publication. He passed his examinations with distinction, and invaded the arena of the college debaters with such aplomb and ability as to capture medals and sorely needed prize money.   He did all this with apparent ease; but actually it was only through the most laborious industry.

About this time the renowned Robert G. Ingersoll was billed for a lecture at Des Moines, and thither journeyed young Albert, who secured a front seat so as to study the oratory of this prince of the platform.   He noticed every detail of the eloquent agnostic's person — his silk hosiery, patent leather pumps, elegantly fitting evening clothes, and decided that these accessories contributed to the orator's success.   He reveled in the Ingersollian rhetoric, but was annoyed by the humorous thrusts, which, it seemed to this youthful critic, were undignified and detracted from the general effect of the lecture.

Beveridge formed friendships with Jonathan P. Dolliver of Iowa and with other eminent politicians — men destined to fight side by side with him in later years.   He graduated from DePauw, studied law, was admitted to the bar, set up an office in Indianapolis, and took to politics as naturally as a flushed partridge takes to flight.

As a youth Beveridge was more admired than loved, though then and thereafter he had his devoted friends.

He was friendly enough, for that matter, but also proud, haughty, a little aloof, and wore always an air of supreme self-confidence. He was particular about his clothes — the tilt of his hat brim, the texture and cut of his suits, the shade of his cravat — and he invariably dressed in good taste. In those early days in Indianapolis, he was an usher on Sundays in the fashionable Meridian street Methodist Episcopal Church, where he showed the cultured worshipers to their pews in the grand manner. " He was a gallant usher in those days," Meredith Nicholson was to write many years later. And James W. Noel, writing to Claude G. Bowers, said, " He ushered pewholders to their seats with the grace of a Chesterfield, and passed the plate as though granting a favor."

Thus the handsome young lawyer became the center of the Hoosier capital's literary and social set, much admired, generously praised, and the toast of many a convivial group. Warmly welcomed into the exclusive clubs, Beveridge read carefully phrased papers before societies historical, political and legal, much to their profit and delight. " Brilliant Beveridge " they called him, and all the time he was talking — talking — and by 1898 he had talked himself into the United States Senate, and from that exalted place he talked himself into national renown.

Up to this time the style of Beveridge's oratory was what might be called " the higher florid." It was never bombastic or grandiloquent, was always dignified and marked by thrilling climaxes. It was nationalistic in spirit, imperialistic in scope, and thoroughly Republican in partisanship. And it was serious, deadly serious, and yet enthusiastic and patriotic to the core. A good example of his oratorical style and content at this period is to be found in his famous " March of the Flag " speech, delivered in Tomlinson Hall, Indianapolis, scene of so many of his oratorical triumphs. The time was September, 1898. He was in fine fettle; his enunciation was perfect, his delivery impassioned at times, yet always under control. He stirred a packed hall to a frenzy of excitement with these ardent paragraphs:

The march of the flag. [Cheers.] In 1789, the flag of the republic waved over four million souls in thirteen states and their savage territory which stretched to the Mississippi, to Canada and to the Floridas. The timid souls of that day said that no new territory was needed, and for an hour they were right. But Jefferson, through whose intellect the centuries marched; Jefferson, whose blood was Saxon, but whose schooling was French, and therefore whose deeds negatived his words; Jefferson, who dreamed of Cuba as a state of the union; Jefferson, the first imperialist of the republic — Jefferson acquired that imperial territory which swept from Mississippi to the mountains, from Texas to the British possessions, and the march of the flag began. [Applause.] The infidels to the gospel of liberty raved, but the flag swept on. [Applause.]

The title to that noble land out of which Oregon, Washington, Idaho and Montana have been carved was uncertain; Jefferson, strict constructionist of constitutional power though he was, obeyed the Anglo-Saxon impulse within him, whose watchword then, and whose watchword throughout the world today is " Forward " [applause], another empire was added to the republic, and the march of the flag went on. [Applause.]

Those who denied the power of free institutions to expand urged every argument and more that we hear today; but the people's judgment approved the command of their blood, and the march of the flag went on. [Applause.]

The screen of land from New Orleans to Florida shut us from the gulf, and over this and the Everglades peninsula waved the saffron flag of Spain; Andrew Jackson seized both, the American people stood at his back, and, under Monroe, Florida came under the dominion of the republic, and the march of the flag went on. [Applause.] The Cassandras prophesied every prophecy we hear today, but the march of the flag went on. Then Texas responded to the bugle call of liberty, and the march of the flag went on. [Cheers.] And at last we waged war with Mexico, and the flag swept over the southwest, over peerless California, past the Golden Gate to Oregon, and from ocean to ocean its folds of glory blazed. [Great cheering.]

And now, obeying the same voice that Jefferson heard and obeyed, that Jackson heard and obeyed, that Monroe heard and obeyed, that Seward heard and obeyed, that Ulysses S. Grant heard and obeyed, that Benjamin Harrison heard and obeyed, William McKinley plants the flag over all the islands of the seas, outposts of commerce, citadels of national security, and the march of the flag goes on. [Long-continued cheering.] Bryan, Bailey, Bland and Blackburn command it to stand still, but the march of the flag goes on. [Renewed cheering.] And the question you will answer at the polls is whether you will stand with this quartet of disbelief in the American people, or whether you are marching onward with the flag. [Tremendous cheering.] . . .

In the Senate, Beveridge disregarded the precious tradition that a new member should sit mute for a year before addressing that august body. The junior senator from Indiana had been given a place on the Committee on the Philippine Islands, and since he had just returned from a visit to those islands and had some very definite views on what should be done with them, it was to be expected he would wish to speak on the following resolution: "Resolved, that the Philippine Islands are territories belonging to the United States; that it is the intention of the United States to retain them as such, and to establish and maintain such governmental control throughout the archipelago as the situation may demand."

And to his speech on this subject, his maiden speech before the Senate, Beveridge gave his best, toiling over it far into the night. Then he shut himself up in his room to commit the manuscript to memory. When the hour arrived for the delivery of the speech, a packed gallery looked down upon the handsome, youthful, faultlessly attired senator from Indiana, who appeared pale and a little nervous. But when he rose to his feet every trace of nervousness was gone, he was at ease, and his fine voice rang out clear and penetrating. He said in part:

Mr. President, the times call for candor. The Philippines are ours forever: " territory belonging to the United States," as the Constitution calls them. And just beyond the Philippines are China's illimitable markets. We will not retreat from either. We will not repudiate our duty in the archipelago. We will not abandon our opportunity in the Orient. We will not renounce our part in the mission of our race, trustees under God, of the civilization of the world. And we will move forward to our work, not howling out regrets like slaves whipped to their burdens, but with gratitude for a task worthy of our strength and thanksgiving to Almighty God that he has marked us as his chosen people, henceforth to lead in the regeneration of the world. . . .

God has not been preparing the English-speaking and Teutonic peoples for a thousand years for nothing but vain and idle self-contemplation and self-admiration. No! He has made us the master organizers of the world to establish system where chaos reigns. . . . He has made us adepts in government that we may administer government among savages and senile peoples.

Pray God the time may never come when Mammon and the love of ease shall so debase our blood that we will fear to shed it for the flag and its imperial destiny. . . . And that time will never come. We will renew our youth at the fountain of new and glorious deeds. We will exalt our reverence for the flag by carrying it to a nobler future, as well as in remembering its ineffable past. . . . And so, senators, with reverent hearts, where dwells the fear of God, the American people move forward to the future of their hope and the doing of his work.

Adopt the resolutions offered that peace may quickly come and that we may begin our saving, regenerating and uplifting work. Adopt it, and this bloodshed will cease when these deluded children of our islands learn that this is the final word of the representatives of the American people in Congress assembled. Reject it, and the world, history, and the American people will know where to forever fix the awful responsibility for the consequences that will surely follow our failure to do our manifest duty. How dare we delay when our soldiers' blood is flowing?

Senator Beveridge woke the next morning to find himself a national figure, with telegrams of congratulation piling his desk and newspaper editorials eulogizing him from coast to coast. There were criticisms, but they were of the policy he advocated, not of the speech itself; that was beyond praise.

When Beveridge sat down at the close of his speech that memorable day and after the applause had ceased, Senator George F. Hoar of Massachusetts, his face flushed and voice trembling with emotion, rose, was recognized by the presiding officer, and spoke as follows:

I have listened, delighted, as I suppose all the members of the Senate did, to the eloquence of my honorable friend from Indiana. I am glad to welcome to the public service his enthusiasm, his patriotism, his silver speech, and the earnestness and courage with which he has devoted himself to the discharge of his duty to the republic, as he conceives it.

Yet, Mr. President, as I heard his eloquent description of wealth and glory, and commerce and trade, I listened in vain for those words which the American people have been wont to take upon their lips in every solemn crisis of their history. I heard much calculated to excite the imagination of youth seeking wealth, or the youth charmed by the dream of empire. But the words right, duty, freedom, were absent, my friend must permit me to say, from that eloquent speech. I could think of this brave young republic of ours listening to what he had to say, of but one occurrence:

" The devil taketh him up to an exceedingly high mountain, and showeth him all the kingdoms of the world, and the glory of them; and saith unto him, All these things will I give thee, if thou wilt fall down and worship me. Then saith Jesus unto him, Get thee behind me, Satan."

On New Year's Eve, 1900, in the Columbia Club, Indianapolis, Beveridge and former President Benjamin Harrison were the principal orators. It was a night long to be remembered. The two Indiana statesmen did not see eye to eye on the subject of imperialism. Beveridge preceded Harrison, and warmed immediately to his subject. Two paragraphs of that speech follow:

Before the clock of the century strikes the half-hour the American republic will be the sought-for arbitrator of the disputes of the nations, the justice of whose decrees every people will admit, and whose power to enforce them none will dare resist. And to me, the republic as an active dispenser of international justice is a picture more desirable than a republic as an idle, egotistical example posing before mankind as a statue of do-nothing righteousness. A new day has dawned. Civilization will never loose its hold on Shanghai; civilization will never depart from Hongkong; the gates of Pekin will never again be closed against the methods of modern men. The regeneration of the world, physical as well as moral, has begun, and revolutions never move backward.

Give posterity a clean future. Stretch no treaty prohibitions across our tide of time. Clear the way for the coming race. Give the children of today and the children yet unborn the liberty to solve the questions of their own day in their own way. How awful is the egotism that would fasten about the brow of future generations the steel band of our little thought! We cannot foresee all the problems that will arise after we are gone, any more than the fathers foresaw the problems that arose after they were gone — problems that our elders have had to solve according to the wisdom of contemporaneous circumstances, and in the solving of which they discovered new powers in the Constitution undreamed of by the men who wrote that immortal document.

It is only fair to give one paragraph from Benjamin Harrison's reply to Beveridge's speech, and to remark that the former president was himself an orator of the first rank.

At first we talked of English rights, but it was not long until we began to talk of human rights. The British Parliament was, under the British law, supreme — could repeal the Magna Charta. We turned to the colonial charters, surely they were irrevocable grants, but the crown courts held otherwise. What kings and parliaments had given, they could take away. And so our fathers were driven to claim a divine endowment, and to allow it to all men, since God had made all of one blood. To write the argument otherwise was to divest it of its major premise. The grand conclusion — no king or parliament can rightfully take God's gift of liberty from any man — was thus riveted to the eternal throne itself. We made our convenience an exception in the case of the black man; but God erased it with a sponge dipped in the white man's blood.

Senator Beveridge joined the insurgents in their widely heralded fight against the Senate oligarchy and the Old Guard. He stood side by side with Dolliver and Cummens of Iowa, Clapp of Minnesota, LaFollette of Wisconsin, Bristow of Kansas, and others of the far-famed battling group. And when the Progressive party headed by Theodore Roosevelt came into existence, it was Beveridge who made at the birth of the Bull Moose party in Chicago, 1912, one of the noblest orations of his speaking career. What a convention that was! What drama! What perfervid excitement! And the songs —

> Follow! Follow!
> We will follow Roosevelt
> Anywhere, Everywhere,
> We will follow on.

And Oscar Strauss, Jewish philanthropist, leading the New York delegation singing:

> Onward, Christian soldiers,
> Marching as to war. . . .

Beveridge was in excellent speaking trim. His sentences were short, epigrammatic. His style was less florid than in earlier years, simpler, stronger, and he said things that stirred the cheering thousands. The paragraphs that follow, even in type have the power to thrill:

We stand for a nobler America. We stand for an undivided nation. We stand for a broader liberty, a fuller justice. We stand for social brotherhood as against savage individualism. We stand for an intelligent cooperation instead of a reckless competition. We stand for mutual helpfulness instead of mutual hatred. We stand for equal rights as a fact of life instead of a catchword of politics. We stand for the rule of the people as a practical truth instead of a meaningless pretense. We stand for a representative government that represents the people. We battle for the actual rights of man.

We found a party through which all who believe with us can work with us; or rather, we declare our allegiance to a party which the people themselves have founded.

For this party comes from the grass roots. It has grown from the soil of the people's hard necessities. It has the vitality of the people's strong convictions. The people have work to be done, and our party is here to do that work.

The people vote for one party and find their hopes turned to ashes on their lips; and then, to punish that party, they vote for the other party. So it is that partisan victories have come to be merely the people's vengeance; and always the secret powers have played the game.

So there is no national unity in either party, no stability of purpose, no clear-cut and sincere program of one party at frank and open war with an equally clear-cut and sincere program of an opposing party.

And the peroration:

Knowing the price we must pay, the sacrifice we must make, the burdens we must carry, the assaults we must endure —

knowing full well the cost — yet we enlist and we enlist for the war. For we know the justice of our cause, and we know, too, its certain triumph.

Not reluctantly, then, but eagerly, not with faint hearts, but strong, do we now advance upon the enemies of the people. For the call that comes to us is the call that came to our fathers. As they responded, so shall we.

He has sounded forth a trumpet that shall never call retreat,
He is sifting out the hearts of men before his judgment seat,
Oh, be swift our souls to answer him, be jubilant our feet,
Our God is marching on.

With the defeat of the Progressive party in 1912, and the fizzle of the Bull Moosers in 1914, Beveridge's political star began to fade. Although identified with the insurgents he was at heart a conservative. He turned to historical writing, and his four-volume *Life of John Marshall* gave him a new pedestal and undying fame. He attempted a political comeback in 1922, won the senatorial primary nomination from Senator Harry New, but went down to defeat in the November election before his old friend, former Governor Samuel M. Ralston. Then, gratefully, he turned to the writing of a biography of Abraham Lincoln. He had not quite completed the second volume of this distinguished work when on April 27, 1927, he died suddenly from a heart attack.

Albert J. Beveridge was not an extemporaneous speaker. He invariably declined to " make a few re-marks " on numerous occasions, when a Bryan or a Clay would have responded and delighted his hearers. He never spoke without the most careful preparation. He never told jokes or employed humor in his speeches. He spoke with distinction always, and never more so than when the occasion was momentous and the setting all that could be desired. He considered his attire to be a part of his platform equipment, and it is unlikely that he ever rose to speak without spotless linen, freshly pressed clothes, and the proper dress for the occasion. I heard him speak in 1914, in Illinois, on a frightfully hot day. He was dressed in a straw colored suit of some light-weight material. His soft collar, cravat, shoes and hat were of the same shade as his suit, and despite the heat he appeared fresh and immaculate.

Some great platform men — Bryan, for instance — were indifferent or careless as to dress. The Commoner's black alpaca coat, black or white string tie, wide expanse of shirt bosom and baggy trousers were a familiar sight to multitudes, who rather liked him the better because of his disdain of sartorial pride. Even so, he was an impressive platform figure. Clay and Webster carefully dressed the part; Everett's elegance in dress was the occasion of frequent comment; Phillips looked the patrician he was; Colonel J. Hamilton Lewis is a Beau Brummel. Bishop William A. Quayle, a fascinating rhetorician, favored an old slouch hat and his clothes looked as if he had slept in them. Beveridge, on the contrary, gave the impression of having picked his tailor with care. His platform appearance was spick-and-span.

In 1912 I listened to Beveridge in Louisville, Kentucky. He took the place of Colonel Roosevelt, who was to have been the speaker of the evening but was convalescing from a bullet wound made by a crazed fanatic as the former president was on his way to the hall where he was to speak in Milwaukee. Beveridge came directly to Louisville from the colonel's bedside in Chicago. His train was an hour late. He walked out upon the platform with a springy step, clad in a dark business suit that fitted him admirably. And these were his first words:

"Not a man, but a cause; not even a personality, but a principle. This is the word the shot at Milwaukee speaks to the American people. For had that shot done the work it was intended to do, yet it would not have stayed the cause. Had it laid the great leader low, still the principle would have marched onward."

Then for an hour he spoke, developing, expanding and illustrating the proposition put down in the opening statement. The speech was a good example of Beveridge's forthright, persevering style. Many orators are discursive, leaving the main road for many bypaths, coming back to the subject after winding excursions far afield — but not this speaker. Sometimes you found yourself wishing he would deviate a little, linger a while at some pleasant spot for an anecdote or passage purely descriptive, but no, he hurries on, the business at hand is too great, too serious, for loitering by the way.

There were those who greatly enjoyed Beveridge's eloquence, yet regarded the absence of humor as a defect. There were others who felt that his intensity of delivery kept high-strung hearers on " pins and needles." In his earlier speeches his rapidity of utterance was regarded as a handicap, but he became more deliberate as he grew older. Certainly no one had occasion to criticize him for lack of preparation or failure to master his subject. As with most great public speakers, Beveridge's style later underwent a change for the better; it became less florid, more direct and epigrammatic.

Compared with his contemporaries, Beveridge holds his own. Less captivating and urbane than Bryan, he was more the scholar and historian. He did not have the musical voice of Senator Joseph W. Bailey nor his giant physique. He was without the charm and genial personality of the eloquent Dolliver of Iowa. He could not capture a crowd with rough-and-ready stories as did Senator James E. Watson, though he far surpassed the latter in polish and wide reading. He had none of Champ Clark's drollery or sledge-hammer forthrightness, and Colonel J. Hamilton Lewis excelled him in rhetorical sunbursts. Yet all in all Beveridge ranks with the small and elect group of powerful orators of his generation.

Albert J. Beveridge is, I hold, America's finest example of a superbly " made " orator; one who was not a " natural," as were Clay, Beecher and Bryan, speakers to the platform born. It is unlikely that Beveridge ever made a poor speech. To be sure, he was not always equally effective, but there is no record of a single platform failure, and this is more than can be said of

Webster, Beecher or Bryan. His shining career is an inspiration to aspiring youth willing to pay the price of ceaseless toil in order to perfect themselves in effective and noble public speech. Beveridge was an ornament to the American platform — that, and very much more.

WILLIAM JENNINGS BRYAN

Oratorical Crusader

XIV

WILLIAM JENNINGS BRYAN

IN JULY, 1925, Bryan died in his sleep at Dayton, Tennessee, but the music of his voice still haunts our memories. It was my privilege to be acquainted with the Commoner. I heard him speak thirty-two times, and all the way from Los Angeles to Edinburgh, Scotland. On three occasions he spoke for me at Central Christian Church, Detroit. No one will dispute Mr. Bryan's oratorical ability. In some respects his speaking career was unprecedented in our history. There are reasons to believe that he spoke to more people face to face than did any other man on the American platform. This is not incredible when one recalls that he was a presidential candidate three times and that during these campaigns he sometimes spoke as many as twenty times a day.

For more than a decade Bryan was the most popular Chautauqua lecturer in the land. He spoke on political occasions constantly, and at innumerable dinners and luncheons; occupied pulpits on Sunday; spoke informally thousands of times. In the summer of 1924, just a year before his death, he spent a Sunday in Detroit, and here is his oratorical record for that day: At eleven o'clock he spoke for more than an hour at a religious assembly at Lake Orion; at three o'clock he addressed a mass meeting in the Coliseum, speaking for an hour and a half; at seven o'clock that evening he spoke thirty minutes in Central Christian Church; at eight o'clock he gave an hour's address before a crowded auditorium in the Woodward avenue Baptist Church; and following this speech he spoke for forty-five minutes to an overflow audience in the memorial hall in the same building. It was midnight when he took a train for Grand Rapids, where he was to fill another series of speaking engagements.

"Beware of the college orator, he's always loaded," wrote a waggish columnist. Bryan was a college orator who won prizes in debate and oratory at Illinois College, Jacksonville. One might say that he majored in oratory not only at college but throughout his life. The inter-collegiate debating team in which he starred had a photograph made in those great old days, and standing alongside Jane Addams is William J., dressed in a long-skirted Prince Albert coat, a high collar and a black bow necktie, his hand stuck between the first and second buttons of his bulging coat, around his ample mouth firm lines, and in his eyes an eager light. The youth in this photograph was father to the black-coated, expansive shirt-bosomed, smiling orator who roamed the country over for thirty years, speaking, always speaking. Having been admitted to practice law, Bryan migrated to Lincoln, Nebraska, where he opened an office. Clients were few but opportunities for speech-making many, so the newcomer took the platform and his oratorical reputation grew apace.

In 1890 he was elected to Congress, and reelected in 1892. He served on the Ways and Means Committee, and enhanced his reputation by a notable speech on the tariff in 1892 and another on bimetallism in 1893. For the next three years Bryan was on the platform constantly, talking free silver to the people. Pick up a newspaper those days, almost any time or place, and such an item as this would catch the eye: " Honorable William J. Bryan lectured in the Opera House last night on ' Bimetallism.' The eloquent Nebraskan, who spoke for two hours, was fiery in his denunciation of Wall street and the reign of the financiers." The place might have been Austin, Texas; Lexington, Kentucky; or Winston-Salem, North Carolina.

W. J. was winning friends and fame, and the 1896 Democratic convention was in the offing. His warm, ready handshake and ingratiating smile were captivating the farmers and small businessmen. He loved to meet and greet the plain people. " What a president he would make! " was a phrase on the lips of thousands.

The Republicans met at St. Louis and nominated William McKinley on a gold platform; the Democrats convened at Chicago with divided sentiment, though the free-silver men were in the majority. The weather was frightfully hot, the discussions were acrimonious, tempers were on edge; furthermore, very few of the speakers could make themselves heard in the immense hall where fifteen thousand people had gathered. At such an opportune time Bryan came to the platform. He had been preparing for months, possibly years, for just such an occasion. "A sweet reasonableness shone in his handsome face and his beautiful voice rang out like the notes of a bugle, penetrating every nook and corner of the hall." * Note the felicity of Bryan's opening paragraphs:

I would be presumptuous, indeed, to present myself against the distinguished gentlemen to whom you have listened if this were a mere measuring of abilities; but this is not a contest between persons. The humblest citizen in all the land, when clad in the armor of a righteous cause, is stronger than all the hosts of error. I come to speak to you in defense of a cause as holy as the cause of liberty — the cause of humanity. . . .

Our war is not a war of conquest; we are fighting in the defense of our homes, our families and posterity. We have petitioned, and our petitions have been scorned; we have entreated, and our entreaties have been disregarded; we have begged, and they have mocked when our calamity came. We beg no longer; we entreat no more; we petition no more. We defy them. . . .

You come to us and tell us that the great cities are in favor of the gold standard; we reply that the great cities rest upon our broad and fertile prairies. Burn down your cities and leave our farms, and your cities will spring up again as if by magic; but destroy our farms and the grass will grow in the streets of every city in the country. . . .

And now the famous peroration:

It is the issue of 1776 over again. Our ancestors, when but three millions in numbers, had the courage to declare their political independence of every other nation; shall we, their descendants, when we have grown to seventy millions, declare that we are less independent than our forefathers? No, my friends, that will never be the verdict of our people. There-

* Edgar Lee Masters.

fore, we care not upon what lines the battle is fought. . . .
If they dare to come out in the open field and defend the gold
standard as a good thing, we will fight them to the uttermost.
Having behind us the producing masses of this nation and the
world, supported by the commercial interests, the laboring
interests, and the toilers everywhere, we will answer their demand for a gold standard by saying to them: You shall not press
down upon the brow of labor this crown of thorns, you shall
not crucify mankind upon a cross of gold.

Among the newspaper men who were present on this
dramatic occasion was William Allen White, the famous Kansas editor. Here is what that progressive Republican wrote about the oratorical triumph of the
young Nebraska Democrat:

From the hypnotic silence which held it, the convention
awoke to a hysteria of cheering. . . . And all over the country, as the cheering continued for an hour, the continent
thrilled to that speech, and for a day the nation was in a state
of mental and moral catalepsy. . . . But, after all, it was
Bryan's voice that won. Probably the peculiarity of his talk-
ing-box got him further than any other organ of his body,
certainly further than his brain. Bryan's voice was a high
baritone; soft, but never quite husky, silvern rather than
golden, penetrating but never sharp. In his emotional moments he put a slow intensity into his delivery; an actor's trick
of dramatizing himself through his voice. In an hour of tumult Bryan was calm, restrained, even complacent. His oration was a college sophomore's assemblage of platitudinous
assertions, but his delivery won where thought and composition would have left him stranded. Nevertheless, he performed a miracle that hot July day in Chicago, no matter how
he did it. The time, the subject and the occasion met, and
Bryan as a national leader was born.

Bryan's physical equipment for the platform was enviable. He possessed a sturdy body, able to withstand the exactions of an oratorical career, such as few other speakers have known. His appearance was magnetic. In earlier years it was singularly winsome — and the Bryan smile, how irresistible it was! His nose was prominent and aquiline; eyes dark, piercing, eloquent. His mouth was wide; lips thin; chin and jaws firm — symbolic of the man's deep-seated convictions. His dark hair, worn long, thinned rapidly in later years. Bryan's figure was good, even when it grew corpulent, though his arms seemed to me to be short in proportion to his body as a whole. He was a man who stood out in a crowd — a commanding presence of eagle-like countenance.

Bryan spoke too often to be always intellectually stimulating, nor was his intellectual range considerable. His speeches, on the whole, do not read as well as they sounded when delivered. His vocabulary was not extensive or especially distinguished, yet it was effective, composed of Anglo-Saxon words understood by everybody. He seldom used a rare word; yet he had a knack of striking off arresting phrases, as when in one of his anti-evolution speeches he said, " Can anybody explain how a red cow that eats green grass gives white milk that makes yellow butter? " Mr. Bryan told a story well and his speeches teemed with illustrations. Some of his best stories will be long remembered; for example, that of the woman who was so fat that she was obliged to get off a streetcar backward and who had thus attempted three times to leave the car but each time to her dismay was helped on again by someone who thought she was entering instead of leaving. This was a favorite anecdote of Bryan's to illustrate his three-times candidacy for president. And another favorite was his account of an occasion when he was limited to half an hour because he had to catch a train, and the gentleman who introduced him took twenty-five minutes. Mr. Bryan put himself fully into the five minutes that remained, and then left the platform to catch his train. As he was being escorted around the edge of the big crowd and through a dimly lighted passageway he overheard the conversation of two men. Said one, " Well, what did you think of Bryan? " Said the other, " Pretty fair, but the old bald-headed duffer that followed him was a humdinger."

Perhaps the cleverest of Bryan's famous stories was told by him in a speech at Chicago during an acrimonious campaign. Fiercely attacked by Republican speakers, the Commoner in rebuttal said:

Some years ago a celebrity returned to his alma mater, a small college in the west. After a speech in the chapel by the visitor, the president of the institution inquired if he would like to visit the room he had occupied while a student. The celebrity said he would be delighted to do so and the two men crossed the campus to the old dormitory, climbed to the second floor, and knocked at the door of the room. Now it happened that the present occupant of that room was digging out his Latin with the help of a fair co-ed — a violation of the rule that forbade girls to visit the boys' dormitory. The boy, suspecting that his caller might be a faculty member, told the girl to step into a convenient closet, which she promptly did, and the student answered the knock. The president presented his distin-

guished guest and explained the nature of the call. The celebrity looked around the room and smilingly remarked, " The
same old table, the same old chairs "; went to the window,
looked out, " Yes, and the same old tree "; turned about, " And
the same old closet into which I should like to peep," opened
the door, saw the co-ed and exclaimed, " And the same old
girl." The student spoke up, " My sister, sir." " And the same
old lie," rejoined the celebrity. Now my Republican friends
are at it again telling the same old lies about me.

As with all popular speakers who are speaking constantly, Bryan had several stock speeches which he could
deliver on almost any occasion of an educational or religious nature, and do so effectively. One of these was on
" Character," and in it he listed some ten or twelve basic
qualities, such as honesty, courage, sobriety, patience,
and the like. As he finished each of these divisions, he
pretended they were volumes and stood them up on an
imaginary library shelf just back of him.

Following the Republican national convention in
1924, when the late Dr. M. L. Burton, at that time
president of the University of Michigan, made the
nomination speech for President Coolidge, Bryan came
to Detroit. I spent an hour or so with the Commoner
in his hotel, and one of the first questions I asked him
was, " How did you like Dr. Burton's speech? " Bryan
frowned: " For one thing, it was too long, and for another, there was too much levity in it. Nominating a
president is a serious business." An interesting comment from an expert in conventions.

To the last Bryan found speech-making as intoxicat-
ing as he had found it in the first flush of his spellbind-

ing success. In 1921 he was in Detroit for several speeches, lecturing and filling a pulpit or two. In two of his speeches on this occasion he used a manuscript, unusual for him, and greatly detracted from their effectiveness. His last speech was of an anti-evolution character, delivered before two thousand men in the Methodist Tabernacle on Woodward avenue. Oratorically he was in as good form as ever, speaking without a note and for an hour and a half. He was argumentative, anecdotal, sarcastic, dramatic, vehement, at times bitter — this last a new note for Bryan. He flashed fire and his arraignment of atheistic scientists was blistering.

That night he asked me what I thought of this crusading speech. " Oratorically you were at your best," I replied; " with manuscript you are a chained eagle. I never heard you in better form than you were today." " Would you mind writing what you have just said to Mrs. Bryan? Sometimes she fears I am slipping." He said it wistfully, and there was pathos in the request. I wrote to Mrs. Bryan, and had a cordial little note from her, thanking me for my letter.

I heard Bryan at Madison Square Garden, on the first Saturday night of that interminable convention when he closed the debate on the Ku Klux Klan resolution, protesting against mentioning that organization by name in the platform. The press accounts of Bryan's oratory on this occasion for the greater part impressed me as not quite fair to the Commoner. True, he was tired, having been up all the night before with the com-

mittee on resolutions, and there were indications that
his health was breaking. He was introduced by Chairman Thomas J. Walsh as " that Democrat whom we all
revere, the Honorable William Jennings Bryan." A
wild demonstration followed, cheers intermingling
with booing. Bryan stood silent, his polished dome
shining beneath the glare of electric lights. Order was
restored after a noisy interval of five minutes or more.
Then his measured tones fell upon the vast throng:

"All that I am, I owe to the Democratic party. It
picked me up when I was a youth to fortune and to
fame unknown; I'll not desert it now [cheers]. Let
me paraphrase an old poem:

> Partisan, spare that party tree,
> Touch not a single bough,
> For in my youth it sheltered me,
> And I'll protect it now."

He received generous applause — and then occurred
an interruption which I do not think was reported by
the newspapers. Bryan said: " The Catholic Church
needs no defense from the Democratic party. For a
thousand years it was the only church there was. We
Protestants came out of it."

Just then a man in the gallery shouted: " Why did
you ever leave it? "

There was an uproar, and the orator, his dark eyes
flashing, glanced toward the heckler. " One thing is
certain," he retorted; " we shall not go to the gal-
leries for a candidate " (cheers mingled with booing
and catcalls) .

He went on: " The Jews need no defense from the Democratic party; they have Moses and Elijah, let them hear them " (cheers) .

He faltered toward the close of this speech, his great weariness showing in his face and voice. It was, in a way, his convention swan song.

In 1910 I heard Bryan in a brief address at the World's Missionary Conference at Edinburgh, Scotland.   In that assembly of notable churchmen from all over the world and of a sprinkling of the English nobility, Bryan appeared carrying a cane and wearing a silk hat, a double-breasted frock coat, pin-striped trousers and patent leather shoes.   Just preceding him on the program a Chinese educator, the president of a university at Nanking, delivered an address.   I can see him now in his flowing robes and little peaked cap with a red button on the peak, a very dignified Chinese gentleman.   As he sat down, Bryan arose, to be greeted by a tumultuous ovation.   He was in fine form, and this is the way he closed his speech: " We hear of a yellow peril, and we are asked, If China is awakened and people are educated, what will become of the rest of the world?   The Christian people of this world believe that there is but one yellow peril on this earth, and that is the lust for gold, and nothing else, and these nations that have contributed of their money to help other nations and give them light and assistance prove that they have learned the Christian doctrine that as every individual can rejoice in his neighbor's good and prosperity, so every nation can bid every other nation Godspeed, and ask it to do its best and be a rival with all the others in all that goes for the uplifting of mankind."

Of Bryan's popular lectures one of the best was entitled " The Price of a Soul." It was really an impressive sermon of an hour and three-quarters in length, based on the text, " What shall it profit a man if he gain the whole world and lose his own soul? " In one section of this speech Bryan discusses the question, How much can a man honestly earn in a lifetime? One hundred thousand dollars? A million dollars? Five hundred million? He answers in the affirmative and then goes on to explain:

> Not only do I believe that a man can earn five hundred million, but I believe that men have earned it. I believe that Thomas Jefferson earned more than five hundred millions. The service that he rendered to the world was of such great value that had he collected for it five hundred millions of dollars, he would not have been overpaid. I believe that Abraham Lincoln earned more than five hundred millions, and I could go back through history and give you the name of man after man who rendered a service so large as to entitle him to collect more than five hundred million from society, but if I presented a list containing the name of every man who, since time began, earned such an enormous sum, one thing would be true of all of them, namely: that in not a single case did the man collect the full amount. The men who have earned five million dollars have been so busy earning it that they have not had time to collect it; and the men who have collected five hundred million have been so busy collecting it that they have not had time to earn it.

With the possible exception of Henry Clay no other American political leader had so many devoted followers as Bryan. He once said that there were thousands of his fellow countrymen who would die for him, and it is believable. And many there are to revere his memory still.

No adequate biography of Bryan has yet appeared.* That by M. L. Werner is readable but not exhaustive. Paxton Hibben's *The Peerless Leader* is better, but neither of these volumes appraises Bryan's political career fairly or adequately. Furthermore, these biographers do not enter sympathetically into the Commoner's religious life, and touch but the surface of his devout and almost puritanical piety. J. C. Long's volume is sympathetic but not discriminating. It may be necessary to wait for a quarter of a century before Bryan can be done full justice by an impartial and able writer, who seeing him from a just perspective will be able to assess his wide influence upon the masses and the contribution he made to the nation and to international affairs — particularly in the realm of world peace. I venture to predict that his final place in the history of the republic will be measurably higher than it is at present.

Bryan was sincerely pious, a devout churchman. Familiar with the Bible he quoted from it constantly, and prohibition never had a more eloquent advocate. There was a good deal of the Puritan in the man, and toward the latter part of his life he discussed religious

* Since the above was written the most adequate biography of Bryan to date has come off the press of G. P. Putnam's Sons, New York, 1936. It is by Wayne C. Williams and is sympathetic, the work of a friend and follower of many years, revealing the Bryan the farmers knew and the middle west idolized.

topics oftener than political. Many of the Commoner's friends regretted his controversy with Darrow in the Scopes trial at Dayton, Tennessee. It seemed an anti-climax. His health was breaking when he took up his anti-evolution crusade, into which he poured the last full measure of his ardor. Bryan's belief in immortality was often expressed in his lectures and addresses of a religious nature, but nowhere more beautifully than in this quotation from his lecture, " The Prince of Peace ":

If the Father deigns to touch with divine power the cold and pulseless heart of the buried acorn and to make it burst forth from its prison walls, will he leave neglected in the earth the soul of man, made in the image of his Creator? If he stoops to give to the rosebush, whose withered blossoms float upon the autumn breeze, the sweet assurance of another springtime, will he refuse the words of hope to the sons of men when the frosts of winter come? If matter, mute and inanimate, though changed by the forces of nature into a multitude of forms, can never die, will the imperial spirit of man suffer annihilation when it has paid a brief visit like a royal guest to this tenement of clay? No, I am sure that he who, notwithstanding his apparent prodigality, created nothing without a purpose, and wasted not a single atom in all his creation, has made provision for a future life in which man's universal longing for immortality will find its realization. I am as sure that we live again as I am sure that we live today.

The Commoner sleeps, strangely enough, in Arlington Cemetery with the military heroes — generals, admirals, and other high officers of the army and navy. From his grave, marked by a simple piece of granite, can be seen the Washington toward which he cast longing eyes throughout his thirty-five years of turbulent political leadership — the dome of the capitol, the tall shaft of the Washington monument, the marble temple sacred to Lincoln, and, partly concealed by noble trees, the White House — the shining goal of every American statesman, a will o' the wisp to a colorful coterie who " also ran."

WOODROW WILSON

Wizard with Words

❦ XV ❦

WOODROW WILSON

THE EXCEPTIONAL oratorical ability of Woodrow Wilson is quite generally conceded. His critics as well as his admirers agree on this point. Mr. Robert Edwards Annin, whose *Woodrow Wilson, A Character Study* was written from the critical viewpoint, says, " As an orator he is probably without a peer in his generation of English speaking men." William Allen White, who wrote a discriminating life of the war president, says that Wilson was " one of the most convincing American orators." William Bayard Hale, first of the Wilson biographers, refers to him as " an exquisite master of English prose," and adds, " Wilson is not only the most intellectual speaker that this generation has seen on the stump; he is also the most engaging." Later Mr. Hale broke with the president and wrote an irritated and irritating little book, *The Story of a Style,* in which he criticized Mr. Wilson's literary mannerisms.

Even William F. McCombs, who was so largely instrumental in capturing the nomination for Mr. Wilson at the Baltimore convention, and who through some unfortunate happening or chain of circumstances became a bitter enemy of Wilson, continued to the end of his days to praise the latter's eloquent speech. In his book, *Making Wilson President,* Mr. McCombs pays him this tribute: "His English was a model of classicism, his strength lay in his clearness of expression. His oratorical outbursts were at times dazzling." President E. A. Alderman of the University of Virginia, long-time friend and subsequently eulogist of Wilson, in his memorial address on the president delivered before a joint session of Congress, December 15, 1924, said, "The culture of generations was in his tones, the scholar's artistry in his words . . . there was beauty in the cadences of his voice and power to arouse and persuade the intellect." These appraisals could be multiplied indefinitely, for practically everyone who has written of Woodrow Wilson refers to his unusual gifts of speech.

Discriminating critics make a distinction between oratory, rhetoric and eloquence. Reference has been made to this distinction in the chapter on Everett. Most orators are rhetoricians, but not all rhetoricians are orators, and a public speaker may be eloquent without being either. To be an orator of the first rank requires a commanding presence, an impressive voice, a magnetic personality, and something of the actor's talent. The chief stock of a rhetorician is his mastery of words and gift of epigram. His voice may be raucous or weak, his appearance unprepossessing or negligible, yet he may still be a success rhetorically. In some public speakers the rhetorician equaled the orator, in others the rhetorician outweighed the orator. Daniel Webster, one of the greatest of American orators, commanded a noble rhetoric, while William Jennings Bryan, an orator of great ability, was not so strong rhetorically. Edward Everett was the rhetorician superb and is numbered among the master orators. In the case of Robert G. Ingersoll the orator and rhetorician balanced evenly. The late Senator John J. Ingalls was a rhetorician of a high order, although his oratorical genius was small.

What of Woodrow Wilson — was he orator or rhetorician? Was he merely a wizard with words, or does he deserve to be ranked among the supreme orators of the American nation?

In the sense that Bryan, Webster or Ingersoll were orators, Wilson was not. He was not a natural orator with whom public speaking was the first and greatest gift. Unless he was the spokesman in some national crisis, Mr. Wilson was not an orator for the masses. He was too intellectual, his diction too finely graded. He was the idol of the smaller, scholarly groups, but never the popular idol as were Henry Clay, Seargent S. Prentiss, or Bryan. In his own circle and in the presence of a group of cultured men and women the charm and genius of the Wilsonian eloquence were at their best. He seldom was effective as an outdoor or Chautauqua speaker. Nor was he a rough-and-ready stump speaker comparable with the late Champ Clark, Senator James A. Reed, or a dozen other able political spellbinders. In order to popularize the gift of eloquence a speaker must unbend and let himself go. Mr. Wilson would not as a rule do this, and it is doubtful if he could. On the occasions when he attempted a more popular style of speech he was not at his happiest.

In his discriminating and meritorious work, *The Golden Age of Oratory,* published in 1857, Edward F. Parker divides orators into two groups — born orators and made orators. He concedes that the speakers we recognize as supreme are of both types, and cites Clay, Prentiss, Phillips and Beecher as born orators, and Rufus Choate and Edward Everett as made orators. The natural orator, he says, kindles his oratorical flame from his blood, the made orator from his mind.

This is an interesting distinction, and there is truth in it, though it admits of qualification and exceptions. In our own day and the generation just past Ingersoll, Grady, Breckinridge and Bryan were natural orators, while J. Hamilton Lewis, Beveridge and Wilson acquired their skill. Abraham Lincoln was not a natural orator. Patrick Henry was. Wilson was not primarily the orator as was Bryan. He lived not enough in his emotions, but too much in his intellect, to belong in the super-orator rank. He could not address an audience on any subject at any time and hold them spellbound, a trick the natural orator can always do. His speeches depended for their effectiveness upon their content, although their style was always distinctive and they were delivered with something of the grand air. Also, it should be said of Wilson that he rarely made a dull speech and was seldom guilty of a platitude.

Wilson's speaking career began early, and closed with that fateful western tour which, despite the stress and strain under which he spoke, produced a series of remarkable addresses. During his student days he excelled in debate and mastered the art of thinking swiftly. Early in his career as a college professor the charm of his eloquence was recognized. When he became president of Princeton University his reputation as a speaker of power and grace grew rapidly. His occasional addresses were events long remembered. His lectures and chapel talks caught and held the critical student body. As an after-dinner speaker he displayed a brilliance of style and charm of delivery that delighted and fascinated his hearers. The probabilities are that without this extraordinary charm of speech Wilson would never have been seriously considered as a candidate for governor of New Jersey. In the campaign which led to his election he proved himself more effective on the political platform than his most ardent friends expected, since it was a new experience for him to appeal to the rank and file in the heat of an exciting election.

The eight years of Wilson's occupancy of the White House gave him his place in the sun as an orator of the first rank. As the spokesman of the allied hosts against the central powers in the World War, Wilson's words marched in battle and were as deadly as torpedoes. In truth, no president has left a more opulent legacy of speeches on both domestic and international subjects than has Woodrow Wilson. Now that his speeches and papers have been collected the miscellany of his utterances is found to be amazingly large, remarkably varied, and uniformly of a high order.

What were Wilson's oratorical assets? His presence was good, though not extraordinary. He was about six feet in height, slender, of dignified and aristocratic bearing. His face was not handsome but it was strong and distinguished, particularly the forehead and the nose. The jaw was long and lean, suggesting that feature of Andrew Jackson. He stood perfectly at ease before an audience, gesturing not often but appropriately. The Wilson voice was not of great volume nor especially musical, but it was strong, flexible, cultivated and pleasing. It usually served him well. His audience heard him without difficulty. It was a good voice without being notable — not like Bryan's, which had the qualities of a bell, clear and melodious, or Bourke Cockran's, which was sonorous and mellifluous.

In this connection it is profitable to refer to Mrs. Eleanor Wilson McAdoo's delightful series of articles, "The Wilsons," published in the *Saturday Evening Post*. In these papers she refers to her father's voice and the spell it cast over the family. She writes: "As I search for my earliest impressions of father, I realize that I was conscious of him first as a voice; the limpid clearness of that voice, laughing, singing, explaining things, stirred a sense of beauty in me, and gave me a vague but warm sense of protection and security."* He was fond of reading out loud, and the members of the household loved to listen to the music of his voice, so rich and impressive of timbre. He read poetry with understanding and with the right inflections. He

* Quoted by permission of the *Saturday Evening Post* and Mrs. Eleanor Wilson McAdoo.

knew how to interpret a word by the appropriate emphasis, and he could shade or color a meaning to a nicety.

I recall a scene at the courthouse square in Bloomington, Illinois, with a thousand men and women milling about the front steps. And standing by Adlai E. Stevenson, former vice-president, who wore an extraordinarily long Prince Albert coat and an old-fashioned statesman's stiff collar and black cravat, was a younger man of distinguished carriage, alert, bright of eye, and smiling good-naturedly. He wore a gray business suit and a turn-down collar. His smart-looking necktie had a splash of color in it, and he held a light-colored soft hat in his hand. It was Woodrow Wilson. Brilliant June sunshine bathed the square as Mr. Stevenson presented the candidate, and the crowd, mostly Republican, applauded generously. The speech was simple and charming. It was as though a gentleman were talking to a group of friends. It was anything but formal, yet it was distinctive. Mr. Wilson, so natural and captivating, said he was probably a stranger to most of his hearers, and it was necessary that they become acquainted. Perhaps he did not look like a candidate for the presidency, maybe he could not qualify on that score, and more to this effect. Then, still smiling, he quoted his favorite limerick:

> For beauty I am not a star,
> There are others more handsome by far;
> But my face I don't mind it,
> For I am behind it;
> It's the people in front that I jar.

Wilson's vocabulary was distinctive and unusually large — possibly the largest of any man in American public life. Certainly he was a connoisseur of words. Frequently he used new and unfamiliar words, or old words in a new way. His syntax was often eccentric, and he loved to end a sentence with a preposition. Thus the famous phrase, " open covenants of peace, openly arrived at." He liked certain words overmuch — but for that matter other orators and writers have their pet words and phrases. Mr. Wilson favored " processes," "assess " as a synonym for " appraise," " movements," " enterprise." " Vision," " voices," " force," " forces" were prime favorites and appear constantly in his papers and addresses. His fondness for the intensive " very " was so pronounced that his critics found delight in poking fun at the idiosyncrasy. His frequent " may I not's " were sometimes a little exasperating.

Wilson's rhetorical style was unlike that of any other American orator of his day, although some, oddly enough, have discovered a similarity between his diction and that of Henry Cabot Lodge. In his fluent conversational type of speech others have found resemblance to the admirable oratory of Wendell Phillips. A southerner by birth, temperament and instinct, Wilson had a style of oratory totally unlike the type associated with the south and made famous by such popular orators as Prentiss, Clay, Grady, Breckinridge and others.

A singularity of Woodrow Wilson's oratory is his repetition of key words in his speeches, a device he used

effectively. In the brief and beautiful tribute he paid
his grandparents in the church at Carlisle, England, he
uses "remember" four times, and "remembering"
once, within the compass of three sentences; yet the
repetition is pleasing. For a more striking example of
this repetition take this sentence from a speech at Indianapolis, September 4, 1919: "Compared with the
importance of America, the *importance* of the Democratic party, the *importance* of the Republican party,
the *importance* of every other party, is absolutely
negligible."

Where did Woodrow Wilson get his rhetorical urge?
There is no need for surmise or speculation here. He
himself has answered this question. On several occasions he bore testimony that it was his father, the
Reverend Joseph Ruggles Wilson, eminent Presbyterian minister, who first taught him the power and
witchery of words, by both precept and example. The
elder Wilson's pulpit English was a model of excellence
and charm. His congregation used to remark on the
singular beauty of his sentences and the clarity of his
paragraphs. Thus did the future president learn the
rudiments of noble rhetoric in the school of the home
and church.

A charm of Wilson's oratory was its apparent spon-
taneity. I say *apparent,* because most of his speeches
were carefully prepared. It is true that his command
of English was such, and his ability to think on his
feet so marked, that he could, when the necessity arose,
speak entertainingly with scarcely any preparation.
The little address which he made in 1919 at Carlisle,

England, in the town where his mother was born and in the church where his grandfather once preached, is a jewel in a perfect setting; yet it is far removed from the type of eloquence once popular in this country and in England and Ireland. There is nothing of the Gladstonian grandeur, the Daniel O'Connell fervor, or the Lloyd George exuberance. But it is as effective and beautiful as anything those men achieved at their best. To read this speech is to get the impression that Wilson was called upon unexpectedly, and on the spur of the moment, inspired by the surroundings, his imagination kindled by tender memories, he produced then and there one of the most flawless of his many brief addresses. I submit it here as a typical example of the Wilson felicity and charm in public speech:

It is with unaffected reluctance that I project myself into this solemn service. I remember my grandfather very well, and remembering him as I do, I am confident that he would not approve of it. I remember how much he required. I remember the stern lessons of duty he spoke to me. I remember also painfully the things which he expected me to know which I did not know. I know there has come a change of times when a layman like myself is permitted to speak in a congregation. But I was reluctant because the feelings that have been excited in me are too intimate and too deep to permit of public expression. The memories that have come to me today of the mother who was born here are very affecting, and her quiet character, her sense of duty, and dislike of ostentation, have come back to me with increasing force as those years of duty have accumulated. Yet perhaps it is appropriate that in a place of worship I should acknowledge my indebtedness to her and to her remarkable father, because after all, what the world is now seeking to do is to return to the paths of duty, to turn

away from the savagery of interest to the dignity of the performance of right. And I believe that as this war has drawn
the nations temporarily together in a combination of physical
force we shall now be drawn together in a combination of
moral force that will be irresistible.

It is moral force that is irresistible. It is moral force as much
as physical that has defeated the effort to subdue the world.
Words have cut deep as the sword. The knowledge that wrong
was being attempted has aroused the nations. They have gone
out like men upon a crusade. No other cause could have
drawn so many nations together. They knew that an outlaw
was abroad who purposed unspeakable things. It is from quiet
places like this all over the world that the forces accumulate
which presently will overbear any attempt to accomplish evil
on a large scale. Like the rivulets gathering into the river and
the river into the seas, there come from communities like this
streams that fertilize the consciences of men, and it is the conscience of the world that we are trying to place upon the throne
which others would usurp.

The address of Wilson in Buckingham Palace when
he responded to a toast to King George, while not quite
so felicitous as the tribute to his mother, has the same
quality of naturalness and extempore speech, save that
the closing sentences have more of the true oratorical
verve, and the phrase, " there is a tide running in the
hearts of men," introduces a peroration of prophetic
utterance, solemn and impressive.

Wilson's address to Congress, April 2, 1917, sometimes known as the " declaration of war " speech, is
generally conceded to be the peak of his performances
of this kind. Certainly it was admirably done. The
restraint of the orator was marked and the dignity of
phrasing superb. The phrase, " but the right is more

precious than the peace," is as flashing as a saber stroke. Even more impressive, and to the mind of this writer the noblest of all his speeches, was the address delivered July 4, 1918, at Mount Vernon. The felicity of the opening sentences is delightful. The flow of the chaste diction is perceptible from the beginning. As one reads this speech today the familiar and lovely estate on the shores of the lordly Potomac is etched by a master artist, the grave and courteous master of Mount Vernon comes to life and with stately grace welcomes his guests as they gather on the broad veranda. The magic voice of the orator has wrought a miracle and raised the dead.

I am happy to draw apart with you to this quiet place of old counsel in order to speak a little of the meaning of this day of our nation's independence. The place seems very still and remote. It is as serene and untouched by the hurry of the world as it was in those great days long ago when General Washington was here and held leisurely conference with the men who were to be associated with him in the creation of a nation. From these gentle slopes they looked out upon the world and saw it whole, saw it with the light of the future upon it, saw it with modern eyes that turned away from a past which men of liberated spirits could no longer endure. It is for that reason that we cannot feel, even here, in the immediate presence of this sacred tomb, that this is a place of death. It was a place of achievement. A great promise that was meant for all mankind was here given plan and reality. The associations by which we are here surrounded are the inspiriting associations of that noble death which is only glorious consummation. From this green hillside we also ought to be able to see with comprehending eyes the world that lies around us and conceive anew the purpose that must set men free.

.   .   .   .

I can fancy that the air of this place carries the accents of such principles with a peculiar kindness. Here were started forces which the great nation against which they were primarily directed at first regarded as a revolt against its rightful authority, but which it has long since seen to have been a step in the liberation of its own people as well as of the people of the United States; and I stand here now to speak — speak proudly and with confident hope — of the spread of this revolt, this liberation, to the great stage of the world itself! The blinded rulers of Prussia have roused forces they knew little of — forces which, once roused, can never be crushed to earth again; for they have at heart an inspiration and a purpose which are deathless and of the very stuff of triumph!

There is a sparkle in the Wilsonian oratory, the wit of the scholar-statesman flashes merrily as he startles the complacent and shocks the reactionaries. Thus in Detroit, July, 1916, addressing a salesmanship congress, he said:

I have found that I had a great deal more resistance when I tried to help business than when I tried to interfere with it. I have had a great deal more resistance of counsel, of special counsel, when I tried to alter the things that are established than when I tried to do anything else. We call ourselves a liberal nation, whereas as a matter of fact we are one of the most conservative nations in the world. If you want to make enemies, try to change something. You know why it is. To do things today exactly the way you did them yesterday saves thinking. It does not cost you anything. You have acquired the habit; you know the routine; you do not have to plan anything, and it frightens you with a hint of exertion to learn that you will have to do it a different way tomorrow. Until I became a college teacher, I used to think that the young men were radical, but college boys are the greatest conservatives I ever tackled in my life, largely because they have associated too much with their fathers. What you have to do with them is to take them up upon some visionary height and show them the map of the world as it is. Do not let them see their father's factory. Do not let them see their father's counting house. Let them see the great valleys teeming with laborious people. Let them see the great struggle of men in realms they never dreamed of. Let them see the great emotional power that is in the world, the great ambitions, the great hopes, the great fears. Give them some picture of mankind, and then their father's business and every other man's business will begin to fall into place. They will see that it is an item and not the whole thing; and they will sometimes see that the item is not properly related to the whole, and what they will get interested in will be to relate the item to the whole, so that it will form part of the force, and not part of the impediment. . . .

There is a task ahead of us of most colossal difficulty. We have not been accustomed to the large world of international business and we have got to get accustomed to it right away. All provincials have got to take a back seat. All men who are afraid of competition have got to take a back seat. All men who depend upon anything except their intelligence and their efficiency have got to take a back seat.

There are those who deem Wilson merely a rhetorician. Some have regarded him as a poet and a visionary who often lost himself in a rhetorical haze. Once after listening to a lofty and rapturous speech by Wilson during his presidency at Princeton, Grover Cleveland remarked: " Sounds good. I wonder what he means." Before this judgment is taken at its face value, it may be profitable to remember that Cleveland was not enamored of Bryan's oratory either, and that with all his great ability that illustrious Democrat and able president was anything but a mystic, poet, rhetorician or popular orator himself.

Reference has already been made to William Bayard Hale's *The Story of a Style,* a bitter little book in which the author satirizes both Wilson's literary style and his political ideals. It is a clever but not a convincing work. Taken from their context the words and sentences of any orator or writer can be similarly ridiculed and made to appear " hazy," " foolish," " inconsistent," or what not. It is possible that had Hale lived he would have regretted this smart and smarting criticism of a man whom he once honored and eulogized to the skies. In so far as Wilson's fame as orator or statesman is involved, *The Story of a Style* has proved a literary dud, although the book itself is something of a curiosity, as well as a witness to a mental dexterity and a clever analytical sense which might well have been put to better use.

The Wilson humor was as distinctive as the Wilson vocabulary. It was usually subtle, occasionally broad, and persuasive always. Wilson was ever witty and quick at repartee. An example of his cleverness at this sort of thing was given on the occasion of his speaking to the students at Columbia University during his headship of Princeton. He was introduced by Dr. Nicholas Murray Butler, president of Columbia, who dwelt on the fact that Princeton, compared with New York, was a sleepy old place with plenty of time for leisure, resting and sleeping. He played on this note so long that President Wilson began with the same theme. He gravely conceded that Princeton was sleepy, and that the president, faculty and students, slept a great deal of the time. " But," said he, " as for the president of Columbia, it could be said ' he who ruleth over Israel neither slumbereth nor sleepeth. ' "   In the uproar of applause and laughter that followed this sally, the great body of students, for the most part composed of bright young men and women who traced their racial line to Abraham, joined in boisterously.

Wilson told a Scotch story admirably — that is, with restraint, the only proper way to tell a story at the expense of that race.   He managed an Irish story equally well, and some of his stump speeches, made while he was a candidate for the governorship of New Jersey, were embellished with these stories, much to the delight of the Irishmen in his audiences.   His love for limericks and his aptness at composing them contributed to the sparkle of his conversation and adorned his less formal discourses.   He may not have been the most oratorical of our presidents, but he surely was one of the most literary.

With the passing years Woodrow Wilson is certain to rank high among the world's great orators.   For was he not a mighty voice crying in the wilderness of the world's most awful war, " Make ye the way of peace secure "?   And did he not meet life with " antique courage "?   Many of his speeches are destined to live, and his sprightly epigrams and brilliant phrases will appear and reappear in the speeches and writings of generations yet to be born.   He will be remembered as a lord of language, a statesman, a patriot, a prophet, a dreamer who died " drunken with the dreamer's wine."

BIBLIOGRAPHY

BIBLIOGRAPHY

IN THE preparation of this book I have made use of practically all of the published biographies of the subjects of my fifteen chapters. Also, I have consulted many volumes of speeches. I might add that my own shelves are brave with biography and that I am, in a modest way, a collector of Americana.

Of the distinguished orators studied in this volume there are excellent biographies of all save Grady and Ingersoll. Full and definitive lives of these two eloquent sons of the republic are yet to be written.

If there is one source book to which I owe more than to any other, it is *The Golden Age of American Oratory,* by Edward G. Parker, published in Boston in 1857. But this volume is out of print and one is fortunate to own a copy. Moreover, Parker's excellent work covers only the period from Fisher Ames to Henry Ward Beecher, and while it is thorough and scholarly it passes over a few great speakers who deserve treatment. There is need of a volume written in the same spirit and thoroughness as Parker's book and brought down, say, to — and including — Bryan.

Adams, Charles Hopkins. *The Godlike Daniel.* New York: 1930.
Agar, Herbert. *The People's Choice.* Boston: 1933.
Allen, A. V. G. *Phillips Brooks.* New York: 1907.

American Statesman. Various writers. New York: 1892.

Angle, Paul M. " Here Have I Lived ," in *The Springfield of Lincoln.* Springfield: 1935.

Austin, George L. *Life and Times of Wendell Phillips.* Boston: 1884.

Baker, Ray Stannard. *Woodrow Wilson, Life and Letters,* vols. 1–5. New York: 1927, 1931, 1935.

Baldwin, Joseph G. *Party Leaders — Sketches of Jefferson, Hamilton, Jackson, Clay, and Randolph.* New York: 1864.

Barton, William E. *The Life of Abraham Lincoln* (2 vols.). Indianapolis: 1925.

———— *Lincoln at Gettysburg.* Indianapolis: 1930.

Basler, Roy P. *The Lincoln Legend.* New York: 1935.

Benton, Thomas Hart. *Thirty Years' View* (2 vols.). New York: 1854.

Beveridge, Albert J. *Abraham Lincoln* (2 vols.). 1917, 1928.

Biographia Americana. By a Gentleman of Philadelphia. New York: 1825.

Blaine, James G. *Twenty Years of Congress* (2 vols.). Norwich, Conn.: 1884.

Bowers, Claude G. *Beveridge and the Progressive Era.* Boston: 1932.

Bradford, Gamaliel. *As God Made Them.* Boston: 1929.

Brooks, Phillips. *Lectures on Preaching.* New York: 1893.

———— *Sermons.* New York: 1897.

Bryan, William Jennings. *The First Battle*. Chicago: 1896.

———— *Memoirs* (Mary Baird Bryan, co-author). Philadelphia: 1925.

———— *Speeches*. New York: 1909.

———— *World's Famous Orations* (10 vols.). New York and London: 1906.

Clay, Henry. *Life and Speeches of Henry Clay* (2 vols.). Hartford: 1855.

Colton, Calvin. *Life and Times of Henry Clay* (2 vols.). New York: 1846.

———— *Last Year of Henry Clay*. New York: 1856.

———— *The Private Correspondence of Henry Clay*. Cincinnati: 1856.

Dodd, William E. *Woodrow Wilson and His Work*. New York: 1926.

Dunn, Arthur Wallace. *From Harrison to Harding* (2 vols.). New York: 1922.

Fuess, Claude Moore. *Daniel Webster* (2 vols.). Boston: 1931.

Green, Thomas M. *Historic Families of Kentucky*. Cincinnati: 1889.

Hale, William Bayard. *Woodrow Wilson*. New York: 1912.

———— *The Story of a Style*. New York: 1920.

Herndon, William H. *Lincoln* (3 vols.). New York and London: 1889.

Herrick, Genevieve Forbes and John Origen. *The Life of William Jennings Bryan*. Chicago: 1925.

Hibben, Paxton. *Henry Ward Beecher, An American Portrait*. New York: 1927.

Hibben, Paxton. *The Peerless Leader — William Jennings Bryan.* New York: 1929.

Hollis, Christopher. *The American Heresy.* New York: 1920.

Kerney, James. *The Political Education of Woodrow Wilson.* New York and London: 1926.

Kittredge, Henry. *Ingersoll: A Biographical Appreciation.* New York: 1911.

Lecky, Robert, Jr. (editor). *Virginia Convention Proceedings, March 23, 1775* (pamphlet). Richmond, Va.: 1927.

Lincoln, Abraham. *Abraham Lincoln, by Some Men Who Knew Him.* Bloomington, Ill.: 1910.

Long, J. C. *Bryan — The Great Commoner.* New York: 1928.

McAdoo, William. *Crowded Years.* Boston: 1931.

Martyn, Carlos. *Life of Wendell Phillips.* Boston: 1884.

Masters, Edgar Lee. *Lincoln, the Man.* New York: 1931.

Morgan, George. *The True Patrick Henry.* Philadelphia: 1907.

Morrow, Honore Wilsie. *Black Daniel.* New York: 1931.

Parker, Edward G. *The Golden Age of American Oratory.* Boston: 1857.

Poage, George Rawlings. *Henry Clay and the Whig Party.* Chapel Hill, N. C.: 1936.

Prentice, George D. *Henry Clay.* Hartford: 1831.

Prentiss, George Lewis. *Life of Seargent S. Prentiss* (2 vols.). New York: 1855.

Robinson, Luther E. *Abraham Lincoln as a Man of Letters.* Chicago: 1918.

Rogers, Joseph M. *The True Henry Clay.* Philadelphia: 1907.

Sandburg, Carl. *Abraham Lincoln, the Prairie Years* (2 vols.). New York: 1926.

Schurz, Carl. *Henry Clay* (2 vols.). Boston: 1887.

Shurter, Edwin Dubois. *Orations and Speeches of Henry W. Grady.* New York: 1910.

Smith, Edward Garstin. *The Life and Reminiscences of Robert G. Ingersoll.* New York: 1904.

Smith, Margaret Bayard. *Forty Years of Washington Society.* London: 1906.

Sparks, Edwin Earle. *Illinois Historical Collection* (vol. 3). Springfield: 1908.

Stillwell, Lucille. *John Cabell Breckinridge.* Caldwell, Idaho: 1936.

Stowe, Lyman Beecher. *Saints, Sinners and Beechers.* Indianapolis: 1934.

Styron, Arthur. *The Cast Iron Man: Calhoun and American Democracy.* New York: 1935.

Thompson, Charles Willis. *Presidents I Have Known and Two Near-Presidents.* Indianapolis: 1929.

Townsend, W. H. *Lincoln and His Wife's Home Town.* Indianapolis: 1929.

Webster, Daniel. *Writings and Speeches* (18 vols.). National Edition. 1903.

Weik, Jesse W. *The Real Lincoln, A Portrait.* Boston and New York: 1923.

Werner, M. R. *Bryan.* New York: 1929.

White, William Allen. *Woodrow Wilson.* New York: 1918.

────── *Masks in a Pageant.* New York: 1924.

Whitlock, Brand. *Abraham Lincoln.* Boston: 1916.

Wilkinson, William Cleaver. *Modern Masters of Pulpit Discourse.* New York and London: 1905.

Williams, Wayne C. *William Jennings Bryan.* New York: 1936.

Wilson, Woodrow. *On Being Human.* New York: 1916.

────── *Division and Reunion.* New York: 1893.

────── *History of the American People* (5 vols.). New York: 1913.

────── *Selected Addresses.* New York: 1918.

────── *The Hope of the World.* New York: 1920.

────── *In Our First Year of the War.* New York: 1918.

Wilstach, Paul. *Patriots Off Their Pedestals.*

Wirt, William. *The Life and Character of Patrick Henry* (ninth edition). Philadelphia: 1839.

Young, Bennett H. *Kentucky Eloquence.* Louisville: 1907.